MILK EGGS VODKA

MILK
EGGS
VODKA

**grocery lists
lost and found**

 BILL KEAGGY

 HOW BOOKS
Cincinnati, Ohio
www.howdesign.com

11 10 09 08 07   5 4 3 2 1

Distributed in Canada by Fraser Direct, 100 Armstrong Avenue, Georgetown, Ontario, Canada L7G 5S4, Tel: (905) 877-4411. Distributed in the U.K. and Europe by David & Charles, Brunel House, Newton Abbot, Devon, TQ12 4PU, England, Tel: (+44) 1626 323200, Fax: (+44) 1626 323319, E-mail: postmaster@davidandcharles.co.uk. Distributed in Australia by Capricorn Link, P.O. Box 704, Windsor, NSW 2756 Australia, Tel: (02) 4577-3555.

The food facts that appear on the pages of this book were adapted primarily from Chef James T. Ehler's web site, www.foodreference.com, and reprinted here with his permission.

Consistent with the random manner in which they were found, the shopping lists in this book are presented anonymously, except where noted and with permission. That said, no connections to any individual persons or businesses are stated or implied regardless of how the lists are displayed. Full names and other identifiable pieces of information about the authors of these found lists have been discreetly cropped out.

Library of Congress Cataloging-in-Publication Data

Keaggy, Bill.
  Milk eggs vodka : grocery lists lost and found / by Bill Keaggy. – 1st ed.
      p. cm.
  Includes bibliographical references.
  ISBN-13: 978-1-58180-941-1 (hardcover : alk. paper)
  ISBN-10: 1-58180-941-7
  1. Grocery shopping–Humor. I. Title.
  PN6231.G88K43 2007
  818'.607–dc22   2006034853

Edited by: Amy Schell
Designed by: Grace Ring
Production coordinated by: Greg Nock

Photograph on page 130 by Dalyce E. Burgess. Photographs on pages 216, 218, 220, 222, and 224 by Jerry Naunheim, Jr.

DEDICATION

To Liam (who likes pickles), Sorena (who likes bananas), Diane (who likes goat cheese), Dad (who likes Bud Light) and Mom (who likes Gatorade)—from me (who likes corn dogs).

ACKNOWLEDGMENTS

A sincere thank you to: my family, for putting up with (and enjoying) my odd hobbies and interests; my parents, for putting up with (and encouraging) my odd hobbies and interests; my publisher, for being interested in (and publishing) my odd hobbies and interests; and you, for picking up this book and—I hope—pursuing some odd hobbies and interests of your own.

The Grocery List Collection wouldn't be what it is without the following people. Gigantic thank yous go to: Mary-Margaret Ries, Nancy Bea Miller, Susan Everett, Tara Young, M.K.M., Kathy Keaggy Smith and Jeff Appel. I'd also like to thank everyone who has contributed to the collection since it started ten years ago. There are too many of you to list here but I am grateful for your help. All of you are part of this book, whether your list made it in or not. Thank you!

And these good folks helped me out with this project in one indispensable way or another: Diane Keaggy, Rosanne Toroian, James T. Ehler, Ben Kiel, Jerry Naunheim, Jr., Mark Lewman, Tucker Shaw, Kitty Fipilele, Michael A. Kahn, Chuck Groth, Kimberly Williams, Rudy Charisma, Jennifer Jacobberger, Michelle Lofthus, Teresa Stewart Sitz, Don from Maryland, Rose McKee, Kristine Rakowsky, Jim Coudal, Daryl Burgess and Jeffrey Yamaguchi. Thank you.

And of course, thanks to the talented folks at F+W, who realized how much fun scraps of paper and smart-ass comments can be: Megan Patrick, Amy Schell, Grace Ring, Suzanne Lucas and the rest of the crew.

ABOUT THE AUTHOR

Bill Keaggy is a collector, maker and breaker of things. He has a healthy appreciation for the beauty and absurdity in small things forgotten: Chairs tossed in alleys, papers found in old books, trees growing out of abandoned buildings and, of course, grocery lists left in shopping carts. His projects are all about the life behind the things people leave behind.

His web sites, Keaggy.com and Grocerylists.org, have been described as genius, useless, inspiring, stupid, beautiful, profound and a complete waste of time. An Ohio native, he lives in St. Louis, Missouri, with his wife Diane and their children Liam and Sorena.

Bread – Cookies

milk – ½ + ½ Diet Pepsi

rice checks
LETTUCE
CUKE   TURKEY
RED PEPPERS
LIME OR
LEMON JUICE
TONIC (small bottles)
WINE
coffee filters #4

TABLE OF CONTENTS

FOREWORD

My grandfather was an inveterate list-maker. He'd write something down on a scrap of paper and would never look at it again. For him, the physical act of writing was enough to elevate the note to a more permanent status in his mind. He'd say, "I'm not writing this down to remember it later, I'm writing it down to remember it now."

The authors of the grocery lists in this collection certainly needed to "remember something now." The importance of the lists themselves however, is something less than permanent, as evidenced by the fact that thousands of them have been casually discarded for Bill Keaggy and his colleagues to scoop up and collect. Lucky for us.

I've been watching Bill from afar as both his collection and his obsession have grown. What strikes me as most important about these lists is not really the people who wrote them, or what's on them, or even the people who found them. What is interesting to me is how, upon seeing a list for the first time, we immediately start to imagine the story behind it. It's like joining a movie halfway through. We can't help but start to piece together a narrative from these barest of outlines, imagining what happened before the list was made and more frequently, what happened after the shopping was complete. As I made my way through this book for the first time, I felt as if I were reading a highly compact anthology of short stories.

Most of the time we write grocery lists to and for ourselves. They're highly personal that way, more like diaries than like postcards. They're meant for our own eyes only and they're written in a shorthand that mimics the way we think. (And for some of these lists, that's a pretty scary thought.)

As objects they're interesting too, and a fairly sad commentary on the state of American penmanship. But more than anything else, it's the collecting of all of them all in one place that's the most fun. The wise-cracking marginalia guides us through, and each page brings us something unexpected, and more often than not, a laugh.

Now what was that other thing I was going to say about Bill's book? Hmm. Perhaps I should have made a list. Enjoy.

Jim Coudal
Coudal.com

1

INTRODUCTION

Making lists is a uniquely human activity, like watching pornography or Googling yourself. (Don't do those at the same time!)

Lists tell us a lot about our neighbors, our friends, our ancestors, our species and ourselves. First, lists remind us that we are obsessive. Or maybe that we are forgetful, I forget. Regardless, lists—especially lists of things we want and need, such as groceries—provide tiny glimpses into private lives. They're usually quite honest reflections of a person. Simple needs, amusing quirks and sundry cures for infirmities listed and checked off.

The oldest surviving grocery list that I know of is from circa A.D. 80, found at the site of an old Roman fort in the northern U.K. Someone needed pork, bread, wine and oil. As of the moment I am writing this, the most recent found grocery list in my collection is from St. Louis, Missouri, circa A.D. 2006, found in the street in front of the Jay's International Foods store. Someone needed lunchmeat, poultry, bread, olive oil and several other items. Almost two thousand years passed between the crafting of those lists, yet they are nearly identical. The basic necessities of complete strangers left behind for us to peek in on.

Most found lists are anonymous—just scribbled words on a page. But we can relate to them. I need toilet paper just like you. You need banannas. Bannanas. Banananas. Bnanans? Bannas. Bananas. Hmmm. More on that later.

These found grocery lists are rare specimens. I have a collection from around the world that numbers in the thousands, but it has taken years of hunting and gathering. People are very protective of their grocery lists. I call it selective littering. Seems most folks would sooner dump their car ashtray in the grocery's parking lot or toss a week's worth of soda cans and fast food bags on the ground outside the store (and they do) rather than leave their list in a shopping cart. It's because grocery lists are supposed to be private. Never mind that all of us have to go through the checkout in public. Our lists are supposed to be private, and that's why it's so enjoyable to look through them—unless one of the lists happens to be yours. Then it might not be so enjoyable, because if there's one thing I enjoy more than finding a lost grocery list—it's making fun of it.

Bill Keaggy
www.grocerylists.org
St. Louis, Missouri
Summer 2006

2

1.

JUST PLAIN FUNNY

your list makes me laugh

Most grocery lists are not very interesting. Milk. Bread. Toilet paper. Very few lists stand out and make us say, "Whoa. That's weird." Or, "My, how amusing." These lists have a little bit of "whoa" and "amusing" in them. But of course I always laugh out loud when I see a list featuring "hookers and blow."

"Oreo B Interdental Refills"—now I don't know what an interdental refill is, but I am sure they are more fun to use if they're made out of Oreos. Also, "bourbin."

Floss Picks
Oreo B Interdental Refill
Ketchup
Nats

Bourbin

Styrofoam cups
CLR
gb. bag
smelly stuff
diet coffee
pepsi

Just what strange things does this person have planned? And who ever heard of diet coffee?

Worcestershire sauce can last five to ten years unopened, two years once opened.

4

CHAPTER 1

Well, uh, maybe they were shopping for fishing tackle and a hair dryer?

- Butter
- Count Chockula
- Honey combs
- Hookers + blow

frozen meals for lunches

spinach

creamer

garlic bread

egg

cellophane for gifts to mail

soup

Aisle 17
- [ ] Ice Cream
- [ ] Cool Whip
- [ ] English Muffins
- [x] Frozen Strawberries

Aisle 17 Other Side
- [x] Bread

Aisle 16
- [ ] Pretzels
- [ ] Sodas

Aisle 16 Other Side
- [x] Soda *diet cream sodas*
- [ ] Chips
- [ ] Bean Dip

Aisle 15
- [x] Pudding! *chocolate*
- [ ] Jell-O
- [ ] Frosting
- [ ] Cake Mix
- [ ] Cake Decoration
- [ ] Chocolate Chips
- [ ] Muffin Mix
- [x] Bisquik *low fat*
- [ ] Marshmallows
- [ ] Fake Milk

Aisle 15 Other Side
- [ ] Flour
- [x] Sugar
- [x] Brown Sugar
- [ ] Olive Oil
- [ ] Cooking Spray
- [ ] Spices

Aisle 14
- [ ] Pineapple
- [x] Applesauce
- [ ] Bottle o' Juice

Aisle 14 Other Side
- [ ] Black Beans
- [ ] Chili Beans
- [ ] Smashed Taters
- [x] Mushrooms
- [ ] Sauce Mix
- [ ] Gravy Mix
- [ ] Marinade
- [x] Green Beans
- [x] Corn (Not Mexi)

Aisle 13
- [ ] Various Helpers (Tuna, etc.)
- [x] Pasta Sauce
- [ ] Mac & Cheese
- [ ] Rice
- [x] Pasta
- [ ] Dry Beans

Aisle 13 Other Side (Ethnic)
- [ ] Refried Beans
- [x] Salsa
- [ ] Bottled Water

Aisle 12 (Goo)
- [ ] Pickles
- [ ] Salad Dressing
- [ ] Miracle Whip
- [ ] Croutons
- [ ] Vinegar
- [ ] Jelly
- [ ] Honey
- [x] Peanut Butter
- [ ] Ketchup
- [ ] Mustard

Aisle 12 Other Side
- [ ] Chinese Stuff
- [ ] Tuna
- [ ] Chili
- [x] Soup

Aisle 10 & 11
- [ ] Candy
- [ ] Popcorn

Aisle 10 & 11 Other Side
- [ ] Cream o' Wheat
- [ ] Oatmeal
- [ ] Malt-O-Meal
- [x] Spooners
- [x] Raisin Bran
- [ ] Bran Flakes
- [x] Nuts & Twigs
- [x] Grape Nuts
- [ ] Other *Cheerios*
- [x] Other *Nesquik*
- [ ] Other

Aisle 9
- [x] Ovaltine
- [ ] Malted Milk
- [ ] Chocolate/Strawberry Quik
- [ ] Pancake Mix
- [x] Syrup
- [ ] Tea
- [x] Coffee (Java, java, java...)

Aisle 9 Other Side
- [ ] Cookies
- [x] Fig Newtons
- [ ] Crackers

Aisle 7/8
- [ ] Girl Stuff
- [ ] Office Supplies
- [ ] Cotton Balls

Aisle 6/7
- [ ] Lotion
- [ ] Razors
- [ ] Anti-Stink
- [x] Face Soap
- [ ] Astringent
- [ ] Q-Tips
- [ ] Face Pads
- [x] Kleenex (Achoo)
- [x] Bath Soap
- [x] Hand Soap
- [x] Ass Soap?

Aisle 6
- [ ] Ziploc Qt./Reg.
- [ ] Trash Bags
- [x] Paper Plates
- [ ] Plastic Cutlery
- [ ] Foil
- [ ] Charcoal
- [ ] Napkins

Aisle 6 Other Side
- [x] Shampoo
- [ ] Conditioner

Aisle 5
- [ ] Toothpaste
- [ ] Toothbrush
- [x] Dog Toothbrushes

Aisle 5 Other Side
- [ ] Kitchen Wares
- [x] Paper Towels
- [ ] Toilet Paper

Aisle 4
- [ ] Liquid Dish Soap
- [x] Powdered Dish Soap
- [ ] Comet
- [ ] Kitchen Cleaner
- [ ] Bathroom Cleaner
- [ ] Swiffer Pads
- [x] Brushes/Scrubbers
- [x] Floor Cleaner

Aisle 4 Other Side
- [ ] Cold Medicine
- [ ] First Aid Stuff
- [ ] Latex Gloves

Aisle 4/3
- [ ] Pain Meds
- [ ] Travel Size Stuff
- [ ] Multi-Vitamins
- [ ] Vitamin C
- [ ] Vitamin E

Aisle 3
- [x] Laundry Soap
- [ ] Bleach
- [ ] Dryer Sheets
- [ ] Automotive

Aisle 2
- [x] Light Bulbs

Health Fud
- [x] Raisins
- [ ] Nuts
- [x] Fruit Bits

Produce
- [x] Apples
- [x] Baby Carrots
- [x] Dog Carrots
- [x] Broccoli
- [x] Bananas
- [x] Oranges
- [ ] Lettuce
- [x] Green Onions
- [x] Squish
- [x] Other *onions*

The simplicity of this game amuses me - bring me your
finest Meats & Cheeses
- [x] Sprinkle Cheese
- [ ] Cheese Slices
- [x] String Cheese
- [ ] Lunch Meat
- [ ] Hot Dogs
- [ ] Bacon

The middle of the aisle
- [x] Tortillas

Meat
- [x] Ground Turkey
- [x] Dog Chicken
- [ ] Liver (Ewwwww!)
- [ ] Gizzards
- [ ] Other_____

The middle of the aisle
- [ ] Frozen Chicken

Spoiled Milk
- [x] Dog Yogurt
- [ ] Syl Yogurt
- [ ] Randy Yogurt — 3
- [ ] Cottage Cheese
- [ ] Sour Cream

The middle of the aisle
- [x] Fake Eggs
- [ ] Real Eggs

Dough
- [ ] Biscuits
- [ ] Bread-like something
- [x] Pizza Crust

Milk
- [ ] Bottle o' Juice
- [ ] Choco-socco milk
- [x] Milk
- [ ] Other_____
- [ ] Other_____

Moo?
- [x] Real Butter
- [ ] Fake Butter
- [ ] Cream Cheese
- [x] Tortellini/Ravioli

Brrrrrrr!
- [x] Juice
- [ ] Taters
- [ ] Veggies
- [ ] More Veggies
- [x] Boca
- [x] TV Dinners *lean pockets*
- [ ] Other_____
- [ ] Other_____

Beer
- [ ] Load Me Up Dewayne

Checkout
- [x] Impulse Item
- [ ] Gay Midget Porn
- [ ] TV Guide

It's good to be organized when grocery shopping (see chapter 12)—but it's another thing entirely to be organized AND mischievous. This one's like a game: Find the funny items!

Your standard, run-of-the-mill, incredibly hilarious PMS shopping list.

Kotex TAMPons
Super-plus

cupcakes

snickers

DREAM

Candy Bars?

STUFF FOR
JUICER
(carrotts - PEAR
MANGO - grapes)

Granola
Vitamins
Soy Milk drink
organic veggies
Coors light
ICE CREAM
Tush Cleaner

"Tush cleaner" (!)

Hmmm. Where to start? With the misspelling of aspirin? With the demand for light shirts with no pockets? With the fact that this is the first list I've seen that includes undies AND fish? Or maybe with the subtle request for a million dollars.

STAMPS . FELT
ICE PACK Undies
LABIES   PAm   PAPER ////
                PADS
Mill Dollars   Cell   LTShirts
Asprins   FiSH   No Pockets
                THANKYOus

Oleo
buttmilk
B Soda

Just 1.5% of the billions of coupons printed every year get used.

8
CHAPTER 1

"Next time you go shopping, please get some buttmilk. I like the store-bought kind much better than my homemade stuff."

Ice cream tends to be the No. 1 item on college students' grocery lists at the beginning of the semester.

hamb.

85/15 ?

hotdogs — beef

diet pepsi   pepsi Mtn dew

Sprite   chippage

cereal

bread

MiLK

corn

Dude, I'm like totally serious. Don't forget the chips.

Jolly Rancher 5

Twizzlers 8

chocolate Raisins $4

Hersheys 11

sno caps 5

The odd thing about this list is that this kid spells better than most adults, although the adults probably have fewer cavities.

BOCA RATON
RESORT&CLUB®

Sunday:

clean house!!
gym
trader joe's
goat cheese
onions
potatoes
baguette
garlic
parsley
asparagus
vine
beer
CKN
marinara
pasta
cereal
tomatoes (fresh & canned)
lite cream
shallot
pastry crust
~~vanilla~~ eggs

MENU:
- Balsamic CKN
- QUICHE - ~~parm~~ espagnole
- roasted asparagus
- potatoes · herb/roasted
- ORZO (creamy)

501 East Camino Real, Boca Raton, Florida 33432 • (561) 447-3000

This yummy list of food was just so tempting that she had to taste it! Or maybe she just put on too much lipstick.

Asparagus is the most humorous vegetable because you can spell it "ass-pair-agus." And it makes your pee smell funny.

Americans eat about 35 pounds of tomatoes every year, but more than half of that is from sauces and ketchup.

SHOPPING LIST ✓

- RELISH
- HAM BURGERS/DOGS
- BUNS
- ROTINI
- BLACK OLIVES
- ASS-PAIR-AGUS
- TOFUTTI
- BEER 30?
- PICKLES
- CHIPS
- CELERY
- SODA
- JUICE
- LEMONADE MIX
- CORN
- STRAWBERRY
- TOFU / FLAVA
- CONDITIONER

There are more than 100,000 varieties of rice.

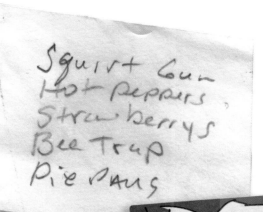

Little Timmy's birthday fiesta was not as much fun as Uncle Lothar thought it would be when he made this list of party favors.

Well, let's be honest, who would want "Pants (the kind that rub)"?

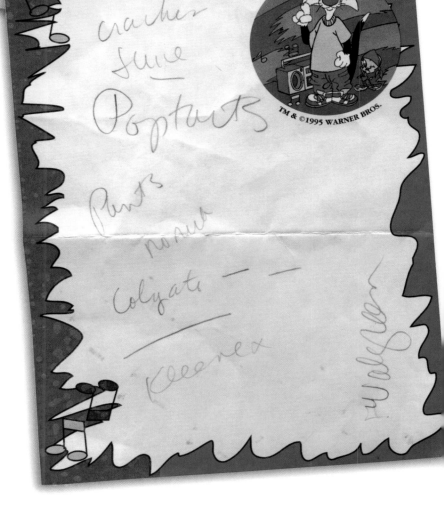

Schnucks

Gin (Tanqueray)
candy for work.

At least it doesn't say
"Gin (for work)."

Baked beans are a Native American invention, historically made with maple syrup and bear fat. It's likely the Pilgrims borrowed the recipe and changed it to use molasses and pork fat instead.

The average American drinks about twenty-five gallons of milk per year.

HOTEL MONACO
SALT LAKE CITY

white bread
ice
van. schnaps
eggs
beer
chips — junkfood

801.595.000

Really, honesty is the policy.
It's OK. You like junk food.

VODKA   LIGHTERS
MILK
ICE CREAM

Cool! A drunken smoking milkshake party.

1 Claritan Liquid
2 Hershey's chocolate bar
3 whipped cream
4 tomatoes
5 onions (white & Red)
6 Beef Franks
7 Hot dog Buns
8 Root Beer
9 Pancake mix
10 sugar
11 Lemons
12 Lettuce
13 chicken strips
14 Chicken quaters
15 marinade
16 sour Cream
17 Green Beans
18 Brocolli Wokly
19 Ding Dongs
20 Reeses Puffs
21 Captain Crunch
22 noodle things
22 2 Lunchables (Pizza — Chicken)

Mega Pack
Deep dish
pizza

sharks
'em
up

chicken
dunks

23 Butter

24 M&M's

Licorice root contains a substance called glycyrrhizin that is fifty times sweeter than ordinary sugar.

Item 18: "Brocolli wokly."
Dumbass, it should be spelled
"broccoli woccoli." Are you
stupid or what?

ST. LOUIS

The distinction between Bud Light and "good beer" is pretty funny. And this list was found in St. Louis, Anheuser-Busch's hometown!

eggs
milk
o.j.
fruit
fresh veggies
cereal
chips
bottled waters
bud light
good beer
wine

white bread
mosquito yard spray

Mo's
6510 Chippewa

$10.00 GAS
2.50 Eggs
2.50 Saug. Any kind
Hamburgg:
Rolls Hamburgg
Hot Dogg buns
(Hot Doggs)
Doritos get 1 FREE
59¢ x 2
Chili
Cheese
2 Coke
1 Orange
1 Dr Pep.

When they ggo to the ggrocery store, I gguess they always gget a lot of hot doggs and hamburgger.

Most milk is 88% water.

2.

EMPHASIS!

blatant abuse of the exclamation point

Sometimes it's just not enough to write something down. Sometimes you really have to make sure one or more of the items you need gets purchased. Sometimes you just want to celebrate the wonder of cheese!!!

Fifty gallons of maple sap are needed to make one gallon of maple syrup.

Lettuce
Moz cheese
cheddar cheese
taco shells - soft
refried beans - 1 can
tomato soup - 2 big cans
cheese slices
white bread

Candy!

PRIMAXIN® I.V.
(Imipenem-Cilastatin Sodium)

Milk (2%)
Bread (Raisin)
Choc Chip Cookies (Yum!)
EGGS!
T.P.
(√ BEER Prices)
Lunch Meat (Deli Kind)
Can Veg/Fruit for Food Drive

Pick up "Drugs"
@ Drugtown!
Call 2 Reserve Hall for party!
GET GAS

For What's Bugging Your Patients
975380-09-PRI

2/12 PACK'S
11.98 APIECE
CAFFINE FREE DIET
COKE !

And don't you forget it!

The first step is admitting you have a caffeine problem. I'm going to take this as an admission.

Cash checks
Drugtown

Need
coffee

* table margarine
yogurt
deli turkey
pulp free juice

butter
lemonade
choc. chips
onions
garlic
basil

→ lighter
lemon
stew beef
milk
choc. milk
apples
oranges
frozen strawberries

A subtle, courteous hint that if you forget to buy me a lighter again I will burn you alive. At least that's how I interpret this subtle notation.

When you lose power to your home, food will stay safe in an unopened refrigerator for 4–6 hours. Fully-stocked freezers will keep the food for two days and a half-stocked freezer for 12 hours.

Well, I like pie too. I like it twice as big as all other foods.

HASH BROWNS
eggs
syrup
SPAGETTI
COOL WHIP
CHEESE
EGGS
POP
DOG & CAT
PIE

ROAST
Pollygrip
Turkey Bag

Halloween

* Swiss Army Knife
  Kleenex - tall
  baggies !

This is going to be the worst Halloween ever.

VODKA   O.J.
          PAPER TOWELS
CLOROX   TEA
MR. CLEAN POTATO
          MILK
          V-8

I don't have a drinking problem. I just LIKE to underline vodka. Twice.

In 1920, 70% of Americans baked their own bread.

A Maryland man once bought one grain of sugar from his local grocery and paid for it with a $100 bill. All because the sign said, "Take as much or as little as you need."

ketchup
mayo
~~Olive Oil~~
milk
~~pumpkin seeds~~
~~bananas~~
broccoli
yogurt
bread
tomato cans
apple juice
cold cutts
miso?
tofu?
ground turkey
frozen berries

Applesauce   1.99

Cold Cutts.

★ 10-inch tube pan (???)

Orange Hummus:

1 can chick peas

cumin
coriander
ginger
dry mustard
turmeric
paprika (mild)

36, 65

½ tsp each

3/4 cup OJ

1/3 cup tahini

3 tbps. cider vinegar

good crackers

S.E. Asian Fish Rolls:
catfish for 6 people (↗ 3-4 lbs.)

5 limes
fresh basil
cilantro

ZUCCHINI!!! (to bake)

SPINACH!!!
sesame seeds

¡Black!
¡Russian!
¡Cake!

1 pkg. dark-
choc. cake
mix
1 cup
veggie oil
1 (3-oz)
pkge instant
choc. pudding
4 eggs
1/2 cup crème
de cacao
1/4 cup Kahlua
1 cup confect.s
sugar

Who loves Black Russian Cake?
They love Black Russian Cake!

1933: Prohibition ends and Ernest & Julio Gallo wines are introduced.

3.

CHIDES AND ASIDES

this note's for you

While lists may be an effective way to record and communicate needs, often a note is required. Though usually used for clarification or emphasis, sometimes the note is to make sure something ISN'T bought. Or it might be a threat from your significant other, a plea from your kid or a reminder from your mother. Sometimes the note may even be sweet and make you smile. Until you realize you forgot the bread.

Large supermarkets can carry roughly 25,000 to 45,000 items. Seventy years ago most groceries stocked fewer than 1,000 items.

Oh, goodness, how many times have I heard that most dreaded of phrases, "If you buy more rice I'll punch you"?

OK, I can think of a lot of other things I might want. Thanks!

26
CHAPTER 3

A grocery store in Oklahoma City provided the first shopping carts for customers in 1937.

CAN I have next time
* pledge. wood floor.
* Fantastico
* MR. clean. or pine sol orange.
* Soft scrub Scrub.

Thank you
MRS. Nancy.

Shirly.

When Neil Armstrong and Edwin "Buzz" Aldrin sat down to eat meals on the moon, their food packets contained things like bacon squares, grape punch and date fruitcake.

"Then after that, Mandy, we all want to go to a remedial spelling class."

Mandy   We all want to Go
          Hy-Vee West for supper

two Lofs of bread
1 - Pakage of hot dog buns
1 - bag of PatoL chIPS
1 - gLaLIn of grange Juice
1 - gLaLIn of skIm mILk
1 - golLon Cholate mILk
    Pop

As of 2002, supermarkets employed almost 3.5 million Americans.

But I LIKE chips with
my sandwich!!!

WHOLE FOODS®
MARKET

FRESH-MADE DISHES PREPARED BY OUR CHEFS DAILY.

Grill

RI

Mayo

Turkey

Swiss

Lett

Tom

Sprouts

No chips

Jessica

place stickers here

Please present this sheet
to your cashier at checkout.

If you don't get the cereal with the car on the box, little Billy will throw a tantrum and the world will end. So get the cereal with the car on the box.

get cereal with car n box

scotchTape 3rd ?
milk
brats
sourkraut 1st
cole slaw

I'm sure this list was made by wife, for husband, with notes on what aisles to find certain items in. Because that husband is like me, and in the past he has come home from the store and said, "They didn't have any scotch tape or sauerkraut," and he got in trouble, and both husband and wife learned a valuable lesson.

I love you too. Don't forget the applesauce.

✓ corn
- Chicken
- Apple sauce
- Broccoli/green beans
- Butter.

xoxo !!

Food - Thanks mom !

☒ pizza lunchable ⟩ no generic stuff
☒ Taco lunchable
☒ Gatorade "Rapid rush" - Blue big one !
☒ Cooler Ranch doritos

I am not so sure this list should have been labeled "food."

O'DONNELL & NACCARATO
Excellence in Engineering
(215) 925-3788

cat bottom
coffee filters.
Gracias!

De nada.

TAPE
COOKIES (WAFERS?)
VIT. E
SPAM
OAT BREAD
X-MAS CARDS

MARGARINE
(IMPERIAL!)

STRAWBERRY SODA
TOOTHPASTE

H.L
. WIGGLE EYES.
. GREEN YARN.
. PLASTER OF
PARIS .

I CHANGE H2O IN SNAIL TANK !

Speaking of "wiggle eyes,"
don't forget about that snail!

Go figure: Mouse-flavored cat food was tested on focus group cats but they didn't like it.

Jeez, how many hands does this person have?

Shopping List

Eggs
Milk
Unsalted butter
Soup at hand - creamy tomato
← get lots OF IT
Mayo

potato chips
BANANAS
lettuce
chocolate milk
cheddar cheese
eggs
1— suet cake - BIRDS exist chickens
= moist!
2) cat treats - Iams original cat food
= Not tarter control

This list begs the question: Why do you want your cat to have tartar?

About 2,500 known varieties of apples are grown in the U.S., but just fifteen varieties account for more than 90% of production. More than 7,500 varieties are grown worldwide.

Translation: "Mom, I know I am a self-centered brat sometimes and I usually think you're an old bag who doesn't understand me and I frequently post to my blog about how much I hate you but would you please get me some raspberries when you go to the store even though you always tell me that they're really expensive please please please mommy I love you?"

NOSE STRIPS

BBQ Sauce
Flour Tortillas
Great Grains Cereal
Toilet Bleach (Clorox white tabs)
T- Island Dressing
Alka Seltzer
Peanuts
Waffles
Toilet Paper
CR & Sharp Bag Cheese
Coca Cola 3/900
Oatmeal Raisin Cookies BIGIF
Hot Dogs 10/10
♡☺ Raspberries Pleeeeease!
Grapes
Tortilla Chips
Cake mix & frosting
Almonds

4.

PAAAR-TY!

this list was made for partyin'

Vodka wins. The Cold War is over and Russia won. Americans prefer vodka to all other alcoholic beverages. At least according to your grocery lists. Personally, I don't believe it. I think most Americans don't write down all the booze they buy on their lists. They get it every time, just like milk and bread. But when they do write it down, vodka wins. Then beer. Whatever the case, the party list is always a cherished find. I love seeing how people have fun. Or at least I love seeing the fuel that leads to the fun.

Why, that's the most un-American drinking party that I ever blacked out at.

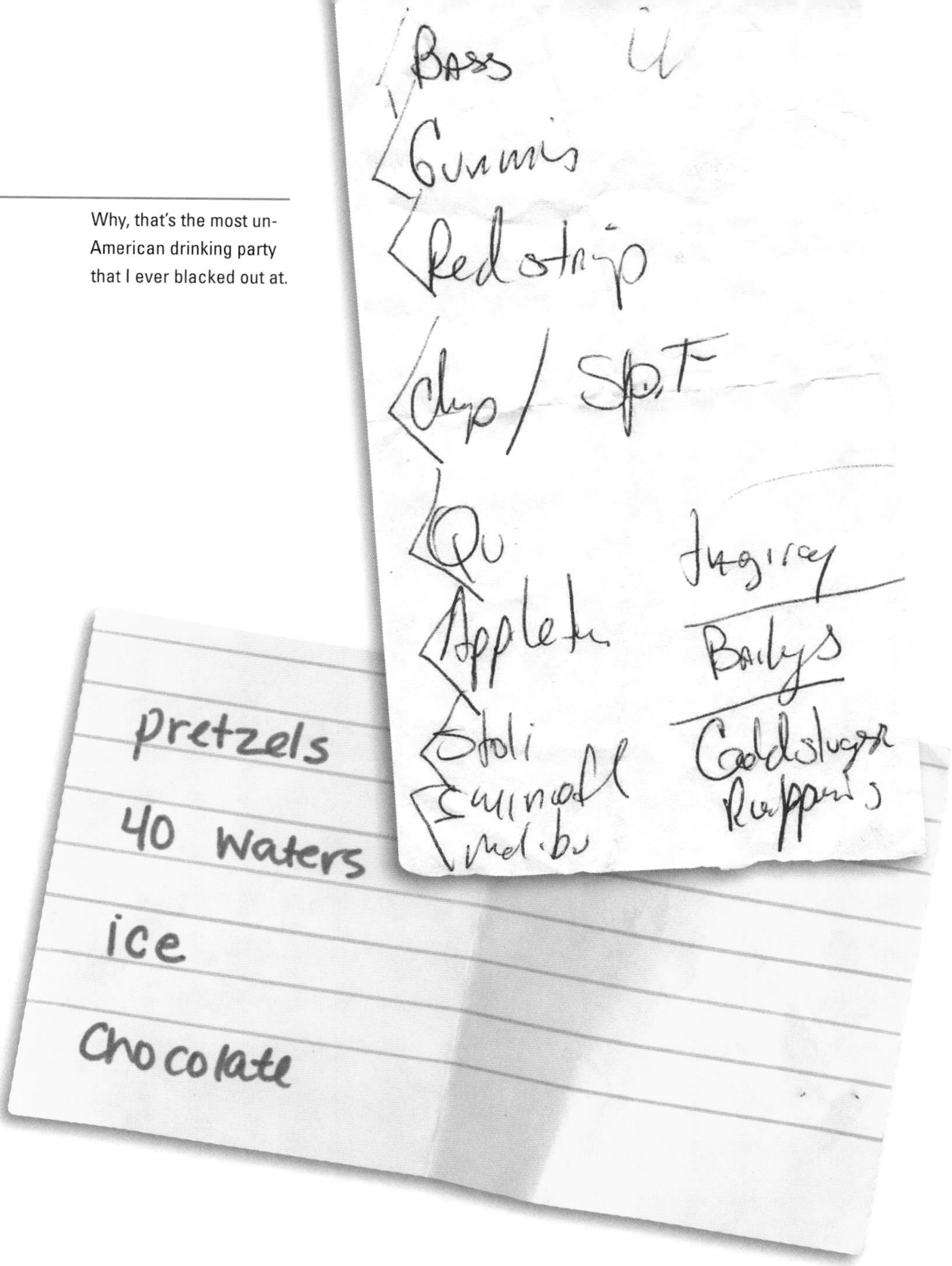

Dairy products account for 29% of the food consumed in the U.S.

Handwritten list:

Bass

Gummis

Red stripe

Chip / Spf

Qu

Applet

Stoli

Smirnoff
mal.bu

Jugiray

Bailys

Goldslugr
Ruppin

Index card:

pretzels

40 waters

ice

chocolate

The lamest party ever.

Calif. Sourdough
Juice
JOOA
Wine
P.B.R.
Jalapeños

Do you remember that scene
in the film *Blue Velvet*? Yeah, I
remember it.

Definition of bolus: The ball of food that your mouth and tongue form while chewing.

Let me repeat that: Buns, vodka, wine, chips, vanilla ice cream and ... kitty litter.

Buns

Vodka

Wine

Chips

Vanilla Ice Cream

Kitty Litter

They must have started drinking already. Why get lime juice *and* limes?

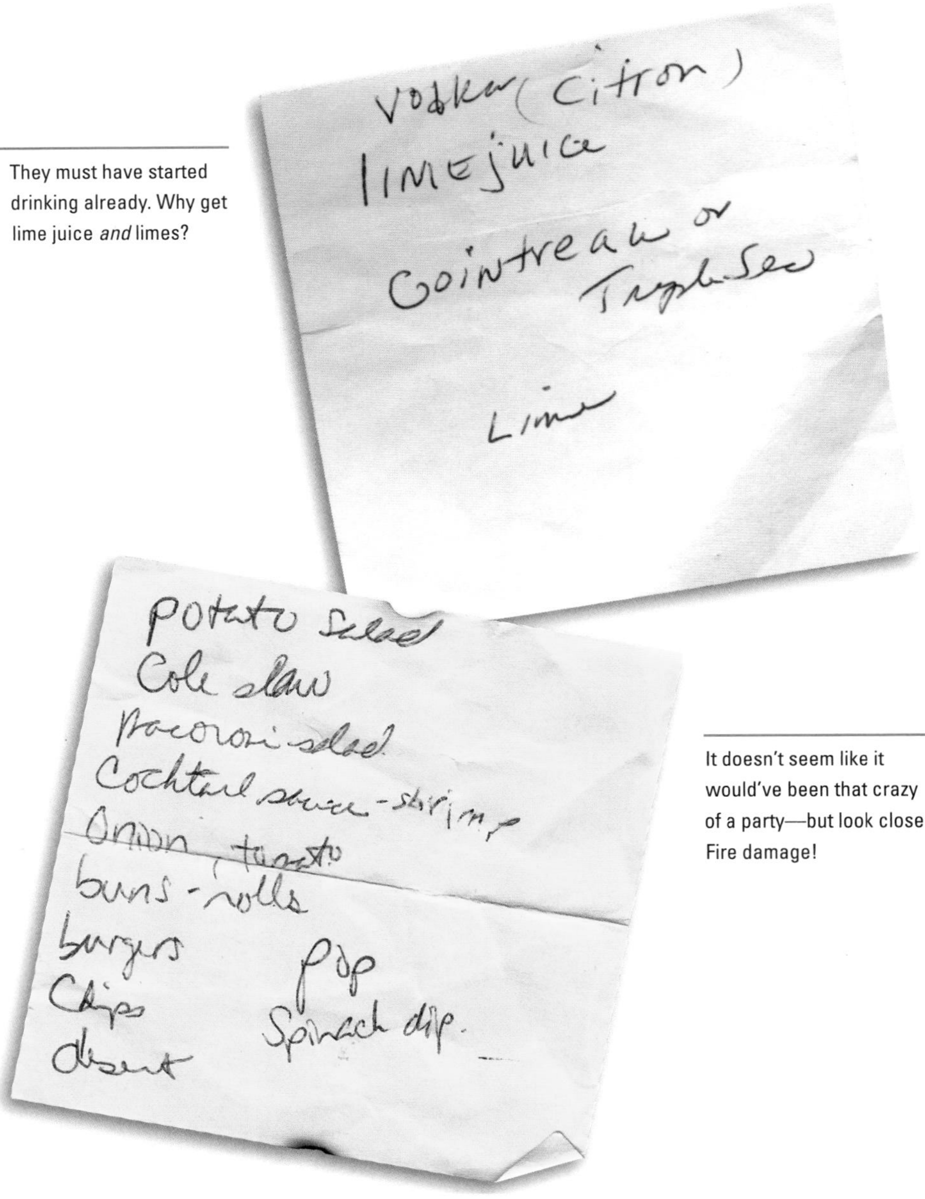

[handwritten note:]
Vodka (Citron)
lime juice
Cointreau or
Tripl Sec

Lime

It doesn't seem like it would've been that crazy of a party—but look closer: Fire damage!

[handwritten note:]
Potato Salad
Cole slaw
Macaroni salad
Cocktail sauce - shrimp
Onion, tomato
buns - rolls
burgers
Chips   pop
dessert   Spinach dip

Knives have been used since pre-history and spoons came along around 25,000 years ago. Forks date to the ancient Greeks, but didn't become popular until the 16th or 17th century.

- Beer
- Charcoal
- fish / scrimps
- veges
- Utewsils
- Lighter fluid

Them: "Hi. Would you like to come to my boring party?"
Me: "Not if you're serving 'scrimps.'"

On average, for every dollar you spend in a restaurant you get $.27 worth of food.

Put the beer, fruit and ice in Ziploc baggies, shake it, and you can take the party anywhere. It's like portable redneck Sangria.

Ziploc
Ice
Beer
Fruit

Ain't nothin' goes better together than hot dogs and champagne!

1) Chicken Breast —
2) Hot dogs/ buns
3) german potatoe salad
4) Bratwurst
5) Champaign !!!

tissues
oil
AAA Batteries

245   50
× 4   175 .⁰⁰
―――
180
175
―――
355
50
―――
405.

Just because you're all alone it doesn't mean you can't get
a party goin' on! You just need the right supplies.

5.

SAD GROCERY LISTS

sobbing over your shopping

Some lists just tear me up. It might be because they just feature things so nutrient-deficient that the items in question shouldn't even count as food. It might be because these lists are tiny windows into strangers' lives that we can't help but look into. You see new homes being organized, older homes that have come apart and children growing up. You see bad diets, loneliness and sickness. But let's not dwell on the sad things in life—let's poke fun at them!

Painful R Foot
...
Diabetic - lack of
equilibrium
~~Thyro~~ Thyroid
weight gain
1 lb per month
1 s T

Small tooth brushes
Denture bath
Tooth paste
Mouth wash

www.MooseCharities.org

Oh, where to start? Quick—
someone call Moose Charities
and get this person some help!

- PROZAC
- KID HAIR
    DE - TANGLER
- IBUPROFEN
- FIBRE-ALL
- SENSODYNE

Wow. Your life sucks, my friend.
Constipation, headaches, aching
gums, kids with knotted hair.
No wonder you're depressed.

Not strictly a grocery list (see, they needed lemons), but a self-improvement kind of list. I wonder how they are doing these days, and if they ever made it to Kentucky (or got new underwear).

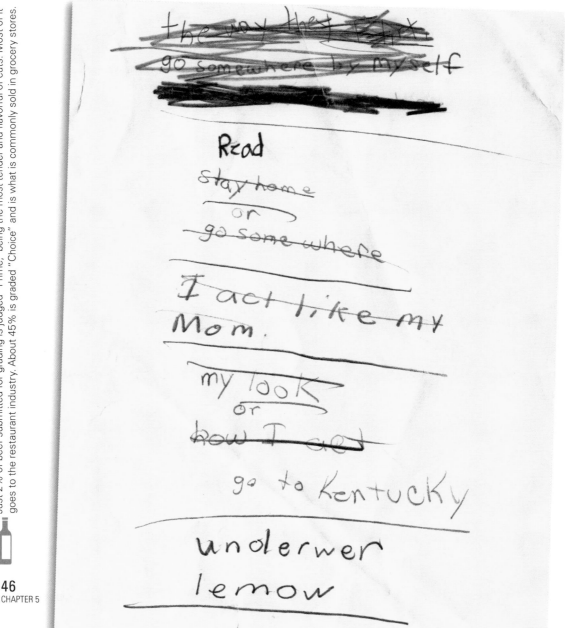

the way that I flirt
go somewhere by myself

Read
Stay home
or
go some where

I act like my Mom.

my look
or
how I act

go to Kentucky

underwer
lemow

Just 2% of beef submitted for grading is judged "Prime," being the most tender and flavorful of cuts. Most of it goes to the restaurant industry. About 45% is graded "Choice" and is what is commonly sold in grocery stores.

Americans drink 2.6 times more alcohol per capita than Russians.

- go to atrium
- buy supplies
  - lemons (juice)
  - brita
  - syrup
- watch tape
  - card 4 dad
  - card for ginny
  - laundry
- get ✓ book ready
- practice
- look over S.S.C.N.
- rebate for Machine
- find plastic Surgeon

This list is from California, obviously.

I hope they had enough money.

1Lb Hamburger.
cheesburger macaroni
Bread
Butter
Lunch meat

if enough
money

- chips -

THE LITTLE THINGS

The grocerylists.org web site is a pretty lighthearted undertaking. Sometimes I blog about organic farming or new food label guidelines, but that's as serious as it gets. Whenever I'm interviewed about this collection, I try to explain how I enjoy seeing small parts of peoples' lives. I am fascinated by the mundane, the forgotten, the run-down and the lost. It's difficult to explain and I usually don't do that great of a job.

But last year I got an e-mail from someone that truly touched on why I value these lists. Usually, our grocery lists are very ephemeral, very unimportant. Much like the one right here that Cindy Stewart from Boise, Idaho, made, probably sometime in early 1985.

Anyway, this is the e-mail I got, with permission to reproduce it here:

Hi. This is the last list my sister made before she was killed on March 15, 1985. Since her birthday is tomorrow (Jan 15, 1959) I thought I'd send it in. She was the victim of a jealous lover. She was a wonderful person, though—a big partier, very social—happy. I think the list was in the ashtray of her car, which is why it was all wadded up. I don't know why I saved it. I guess I just didn't want to let any of her go.

Teresa
Boise, Idaho

List
1) Q-tips
2) Sponges
3) trash bags
4) tomatoes
5) avocados
6) shrooms
7) lettuce
8) Pears soap
9) Sprouts
10) bleach T.P.
11) bread
12) O.J.

Even Create-A-Meal and TV dinners have to come out. You eat, wipe your mouth, then wipe your butt. It's the cycle of life.

napkins
t tissue
Create a meal
TV dinners

Things we need for the house:

1. Pine soul
2. Papper towels
3. Joilet papper
4. Detergant liquet
5. Dish wash liquet
6. Forbreeze
7. shampoo / condisoner
8. soup
9. Pads (for me)

Get mony order for one Electric bill
$23·14 ↑
$8·00 Birth certefile

CMAZ0015

You gotta have soul to get through tough times. Pine Soul. It's obvious someone starting a new home, with a new baby, made this list. I hope they're doing OK. And I hope the school the mom went to has been demolished.

Certain carbohydrates in beans are a source of flatulence.
Anasazi beans contain less than 25% of these gas-causing carbs.

3 U St Reds
lightle bick
Bottle
soda
Gum

3 USA Reds shorts
little b/c
soda
Gum

Don't make me repeat myself,
young man! Oh, wait …

I can just picture the nice lady who wrote this. Her husband died and her children moved away. She goes to the grocery to get some food and a "Miss You" card.

flour fruit Ace - hose
"Miss you" card   holder
foil
salad dressing
milk
spaghetti
sherry

Therma heat

3 pills —
Cosopt
Dilantin
Pottassium

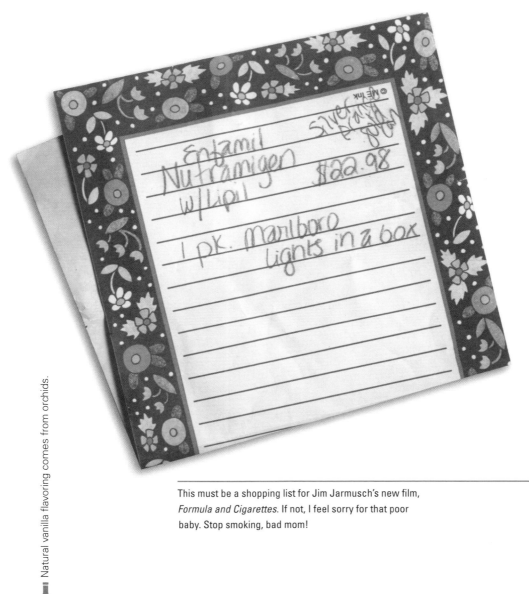

Enfamil
Nutramigen
w/Lipil
$22.98

1 pk. Marlboro
lights in a box

This must be a shopping list for Jim Jarmusch's new film, *Formula and Cigarettes*. If not, I feel sorry for that poor baby. Stop smoking, bad mom!

Natural vanilla flavoring comes from orchids.

"Sprinkle with pepper and serve" is the last step in a recipe for diced pork and apples from the world's oldest surviving cookbook, *De Re Coquinaria* ("On Cookery"), attributed to the 1st-century Roman, Apicius.

silver polish
Bread
Grape juice
table cloth

(BACK)

This list looks normal enough: Polish the silver for a little get-together and have some snacks on the nice new tablecloth. But wait, what's on the other side of this list? Oh my God! It's a do-over! They have to open the grave and have another wake for the do-over.

Beauvais
Manor ON THE PARK   Allan

Excellence in
Residential, Intermediate
and Alzheimer's Care
(314) 771-2990

No charge from
funeral home
$345. - charge for
opening grave

(FRONT)

6.

BADD SPELLRS

the sorry state of America's education system

Wow. You people can't spell. I can spell. Heck, I wrote this book and spellt everything mysefl. But most people can't spell. At least the ones that write grocery lists.

Investors Title Company

219 S. Central, Clayton, Mo. 63105 - 862-0303

hamberger   carrots
Buns
fries
veggie
mushroom
cheess
fudge
Carmel
Strawberries

5224 S. Lindbergh, St. Louis, MO 63126.............................849-0400
5419 Southfield Center, St. Louis, MO 63123......................729-1333
2770 N. Hwy. 67, St. Louis, MO 63033...............................839-4000
12462 St. Charles Rock Rd., Bridgeton, MO 63044.............739-3106
1641 Clarkson Rd., Chesterfield, MO 63017.......................530-1990
571-73 Jefferson, St. Charles, MO 63301............................946-5533
2101 Bluestone Ste. 110, St. Charles, MO 63303................916-1722
230 Mid-Rivers Center, St. Peters, MO 63376....................928-8815
12287 Olive Blvd., Creve Coeur, MO 63141........................878-6255
1006 Schnucks Woodsmill, Chesterfield, MO 63017............230-5900
4248 Forest Park, St. Louis, MO 63108................................535-1600

Add a tablespoon of oil to the water when cooking rice so the grains don't stick together.

Yikes! Almost half the words on this list are misspelled.

I think this impressive specimen may be the emergence of an alternative version of the English language, rather than just a bunch of misspellings.

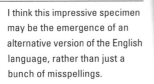

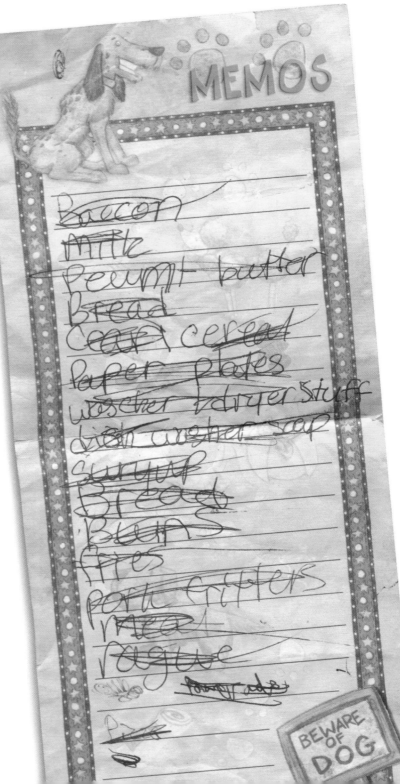

"Busquit." Wins a prize for
most pathetic attempt at
spelling Bisquick.

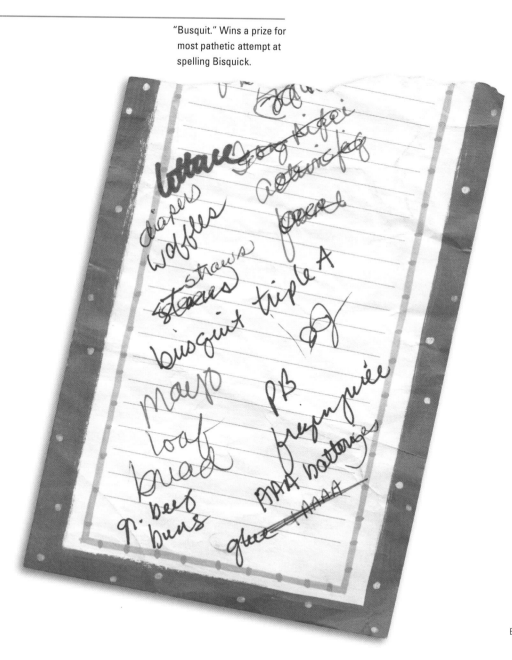

In 1974 Marsh's Supermarket in Troy, Ohio, first used Universal Product Codes and the accompanying UPC scanners to scan the bar codes, which were patented in 1952.

Pork stake? Maybe they're going to slay some vampire pigs!

ribs tip
groun beef
pork stake
juice
RF spaghtte
can souce
onion
red p
hot Dog
hot souce
sweet picker relash
slick marqin

Winston ct
ivary liqund
towel p
stamps
zest soap

Yu Ban Coffee
Box Sugar

mayo
BRead
Lunch meat

PeppSi

FRoZeN Food
cookies
cegReol
MilK

While I can appreciate the attempt to provide some visual balance to the word cereal, symmetry is not really important when it comes to spelling.

TOP
SOIL

Milk
Yoplait Yogurt,
Hy Vee Ice Cream
Strawberries
Coffee Creamer
Potatoe Chips
Adlo Dr Pepper
Lunch Meat — Turkey

Cheese
Hy Vee Frozen Potatoe
Freschetta Pizza,
Healthy Choce T.V Dinners ②
Hy Vee Apple Juice
Mushrooms
Country Fare Cottage or Hy Vee
Baby Carrott.
Tomato Juice   Garden Salad Hy Vee

"Potatoe." The Dan Quayle Effect: I'd say that half the
population of the U.S. is just as intelligent as the former
vice president. And that's scary.

"Tomatos." The other half of the population is not quite as smart as ol' Danny boy.

ToMaTos – 5 CaNs.
Light BulbS – 60 watt
Rib-Eye-SteaK – No.2
ONioNS. – yellow SteaKS
Brat BuNS – 6 ct

Berry Br. Bars
choc Milk + Bread
ham slices 2 lettuce
Potataoes
chips
cookies
Dish Soop
cashews nuts
Toothpaste
hambeger

"Potataoes." And, sadly, some people are even dumber than the entire population of the U.S. and Dan Quayle.

Food poisoning kills 5,000 Americans every year and makes at least 70,000,000 ill in some way. Eggs, unwashed produce and rotten meat get most of the blame.

Try delicious Creakers, the cracker best enjoyed ...
in a haunted house! [Cue rimshot sound.]

Sager
Creakers
Green tea
Carmex
Ice cream
Topping

Linda Shampoo
Rasbury

Popcycles. They're cold—and fast!

Au Gratin potatoes (Betty Crocker) no Ham
milk
chips
pop cycles
ice cream sandwiches
mozzarella (soy.)
pepperoni (2)
cheddar cheese (soy.)
Fudge bread
2# Hamburger
wieners

It's bad enough that you drink so much soda, but at least throw the bottles in the trash when you're done!

ice cream
Pop (Litter)
Diet Mt. Dew
Sprite
Coke
Root beer
Napkins

Nancy Green played the part of Aunt Jemima for thirty years until a car accident ended her life in 1923.

BANANAS MAKE YOU STUPID

Here, compiled for the first time ever, are the words that give Americans the most trouble when making a grocery list. Take a look. This chapter contains undeniable evidence that bananas make you stupid.

Most frequently misspelled words on America's grocery lists:

1. Banana (banna, bananna, etc.)
2. Tomato (tomatoe) vs. tomatoes (tomatos)
3. Yogurt (yogert, yougart, etc.)
4. Potato (potatoe) vs. potatoes (potatos)
5. Mayonnaise (mayonase, mayonaisse, etc.)
6. Spaghetti (spagetti, spegeti, etc.)
7. Margarine (margrine)
8. Broccoli (brocolli)
9. Carrots (carrotts)
10. Raspberries (rasberries)
11. Marshmallows (marshmellows)
12. Hamburger (hamberger)
13. Sausage (sausuage)
14. Chili (chilli)
15. Prescription (perscription)
16. Pickles (pickels)
17. Paper (papper)
18. Popsicles (popcicals)
19. Febreze (Fabreeze)
20. Sauce (sause)

"Bnana." I tallied your bnana
and it's time for you to go home!

celery - 3
leeks - 1
OJ - 4
Cue's 4-6
BANNas

"Bannas." No, sorry. Maybe if you're a three-year-old.

m
g
ccripy
rkts
Propane 2
☑ bannes
☐ Apples
☑ Chip

"Bannes." And there's no "E" in "dumbass," either.

Most foods take three to four hours to digest, but white rice has such a low fiber content it only takes one hour.

"Banans." So close, yet so stupid.

Bread
Banans Steak
Oranges 2 hamberger
ice cream
2 milk
olive oil

Keep thinking, keep interested,
keep praying, keep dreaming.

Derman

Burgens
Broccolie
sulad
rasbury & blue yigurt
bannans

"Bannans." The extra "N" doesn't quite
make up for the missing "A." Try again.

Bananas do not grow on trees. The banana plant is a gigantic herb.

Americans eat 30 pounds of bananas a year, per capita.

"Banansns?" Hmmm. They knew they didn't get it right the first time, so they made sure to screw it up royally the second time.

MILK
CUTTACE CHEESE
BANAN8IS
YOGERRET

Cossee
PLedge
Cup
KACUP
POPCORN

One of the few words in the English language where you actually have options—ketchup or catsup—and you have to go and be like, "No, I want to spell it my way."

BRASSTOWN VALLEY

Georgia's Mountain Resort

Eggs
Mayonaise
Bread
O. J.
Potatoes
Butter
chicken
ground beef
mix veg

Young Harris, GA 30582
706 379 9900

No doubt about it, mayonnaise is difficult to spell.

Toga shells. They must be having a toga party.

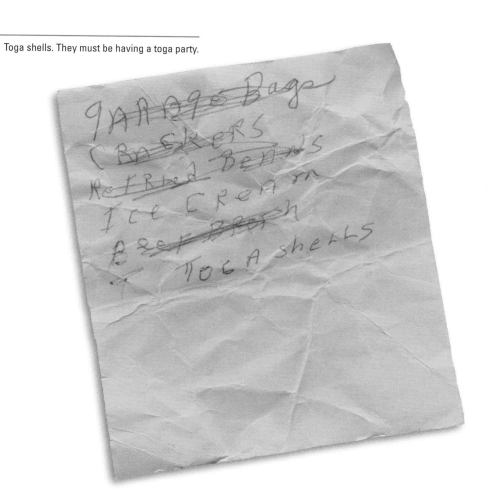

Backing Soda
Moet cleese,
Brownie mix
Bread
milk
Tomato Sauce
Enclalada Sauce
Coke
onion
Potato
chedar chese
Bananas
Strawberries
yogert
cereal

Lemons
grapes
Strawberries
peppers
onions
zucchini

carrots
Asparagus
White
Bread
Yohurt
frozen
raspberries
tofutti

"Yogert." It seems like that could
be correct, but it's not. Loser.

"Yohurt." The losers are all
standing to my left. Go join them.

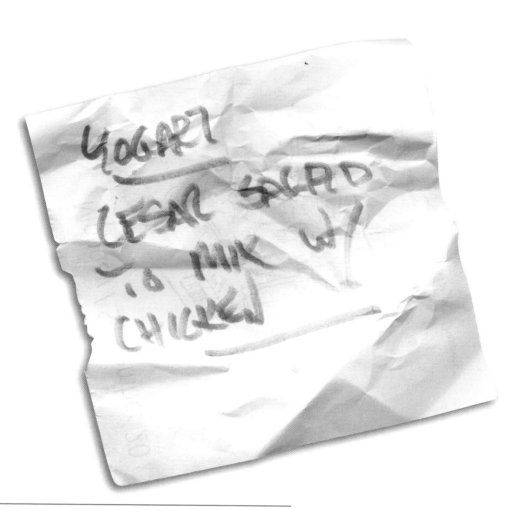

"Yogart." It seems slightly more
likely that this could be correct,
but it's still not. Loser.

"Yougart." And YOU are a loser too.

AT LEAST THEY SPELLED MSG RIGHT

Worst speller ever? Someone new to the English language? Just a person having fun with the mundane task of grocery shopping? Or a cruel joke played on the dorky guy that collects lost grocery lists? You be the judge.

NYEQWIL
SHRIMPS
ROST - BEFE -
BUTER
PRETSILS
BURD FUDE
MAUL - FYLE
CHARCO LITER
FRESER BAGS
CLENE X TP-PT
HARE SOPE
WYPES
DRIER SHETES
LONDRI SOPE
MSG
KRAKERS -
SOTA POP
BIRF DAY KARD
COKS KORNER

Doh! You got the hard ones right: Potatoes, yogurt, bananas. But you totally screwed up vinegar. And beans.

Potatoes
Bananas
Soups.
Vinigar
Yogut
All-Bran
Buttermilk
beens

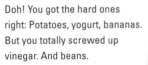

Menu du Jour.
wheatthinsoriginal
toiletpaper

Coffee

I have to give them credit. They realized their mistake and fixed it.

Cherries should be stored at 35° F but taste best if eaten at room temperature.

Sauguage. Sog wedge. Sowgooedge. Sawgwegge. So many possibilities!

Notes

~~bananas~~

Milk
~~Bread~~
~~potatoes 10 lbs~~
~~Bananas~~
cough drops
All Brand
~~Total~~
~~Beef stew~~ (2)
box dinners
~~Kit Kare~~
~~stew meat~~
~~Egg Noodles~~
2 ~~Beef broth~~
~~Turey Roost~~
~~Sauguage patties~~
Ripe Tomato
~~lunch meat~~

If I were going to spell tortilla phonetically, I'd go with "torteeuh."

America's per capita consumption of beef is about sixty-five pounds per year.

4 Bananas
3 apples
3 or 4 fresh peaches
tortias
salsa
Balony luncmeat
Ham lunch meat
cheese for tortias
Fudge Brownes
Candy corn
Peanuts
small sweet pickles

1 milk
1 orange juice
Bread
Cookies
poted meat for lunch

When you think about it, this is a genius idea. Why not combine the two sorry tasks of cleaning your bowels and cleaning your toilet bowls. Use Toilet Bowl Cleaner!

Rum
Wine
Zip lock bags
Film
@
Talet bowl cleaner

HOCKS
SMIMPLY ORANGE
FLOUR — BISQUICK
SUGAR
PaFFS

"Smimply Orange?" Smimply smtupid.

7.

THE GROCER'S APOSTROPHE

not just for grocers anymore

Like New Coke, the grocer's apostrophe is part of the dustbin of grocery history. Most stores are owned by large corporations with graphic guidelines and professionally produced signage. But in ancient times (the last 100 years), owners and employees of local groceries would hand-letter signs for sales and specials every day. Inevitably, they used apostrophes when pluralizing. Oh, the good old days. These days, some shoppers work hard to keep the grocer's apostrophe alive—while grammar teachers everywhere weep quietly in dark rooms.

I love's me some taco's. Everyone who's know's me know's that!

Polish boy's. WTF?!

10# BANANA'S
Pototoes 98¢
CATALoupe 98¢
QuiLLISA Cheese 195¢
TOMATOES 4 — 49¢ A LB.
FLOUR TORTILLA'S 2 PKg
ORANGES 10 LB BAG 98¢

Wyoming
1(800)856-4398

Wisconsin
1(800)242-1060

It's a bananapostrophe and
a tortillapostrophe spotted
together for the first time!

It is rumored that the oldest known recipe is for beer.

Triplicate! Good job! Or, one,
two, three strikes—you're out.

cat food
water
Quick
Applesauce
Cereals
Oreo's
Pringle's

Pork Steak
Bread
Cr. cheese

Steak + Potatoes + cr. beans burnt biscuits -

cereal
Lettuce
cucumbers
tomato's
Kohl's wipes
celery Heat. Pad

Two out of four; that's 50%
correct. You flunk shopping.

It's not Cherrio's, it's Cheerios. Millions of
dollars in marketing and branding shot to hell.

Heritage CARE CENTER

501 South Kentucky Avenue • Mason City, IA 50401

Prunes

Milk

Bran Flakes

Cherrio's

Pie

Coffee

The blue-green veins in blue cheese are mold—Penicillium roqueforti, Penicillium glaucum or another variation. Originally, it was a result of the cheese being produced in caves where the mold grew naturally. Unlike on bread, the mold spores made the cheese taste better.

2 lb Hamburger

1 box Potato stragnoff

1 sugar

1 milk

2 hot dog's

10 Top Ramen

Sodas

2 cig

1 cerel

1923: Welch's Grape Jelly is introduced.

snacks
potatoe's
c'antalope
bagels
cereal

Oh! C'mon!

CHOP'S (H) COUPON

PAPER TOWES
PIZZA
LAY's CHIP's-FRITO's
SNACK-BRR's-DEbbIES
BLOCK 2.97 CHEESE-SLICES KRAFT 2.79 16%
VEGITABLE OIL-CRISCO
CAN's - STAMP's

I'm guessing 78% of this person's life is spent adding apostrophes where none should be.

8.

CREATIVE RECYCLING

notepads are for losers

Why use notepaper when you can use scrap wood, an old piece of cardboard box, a losing lottery ticket or your 2001 tax form? Actually, it is a good idea to recycle when making your grocery list—despite the peculiar abundance of notepads that tout the wondrous effects of strangely named pharmaceuticals. Some tips: Use the back of a junk mail envelope. Use the back of ANYTHING. Just don't use a notepad or envelope with your name on it, or anything that contains private information—because then I will know your credit card number and that you don't know how to spell Danish Rolls (I'm talking to you, Donald M. from St. Louis!).

OK, so now that you've wasted your money on another losing lottery ticket, maybe you should buy your family some food.

The funny thing is, all of these beers cost more than $5 for a six-pack.

Bouillon cubes were first sold commercially in 1882 so poor people who could not afford meat could make more nutritious soups.

See? You can use just about anything, even the tag from an item of clothing.

Both Bucyrus, Ohio, and Sheboygan, Wisconsin, claim to be the Bratwurst Capital of the World.

If I were this person, the first thing I'd put on my list of things to buy would be "PAPER!" This wooden specimen was found at an organic farm. Of course.

If you work for your town's Municipal Authority and you're in charge of financial statements to be used as exhibits in a court case, maybe you shouldn't use those documents to make your grocery list, then leave them at the store. Just maybe.

EXHIBIT "B"

Increase
or
(Decrease)

0.00
0.00
(30,298.61)

$ (30,298.61)

$ 0.00
(984.91)
(3,945.77)
1,466.27
125.00
119.00
89.71
5.00
6.00
(127.50)

$ (3,247.20)

$ (27,051.41)

168,792.42

$ 141,741.01

Every American eats, on average, sixty pounds of bread a year.

OJ juice
skim milk
whole milk
3 tomatoes
apples
Bananas
grapefruit
avacado

Veg.

1 Cooked chn.
3 salmon pieces
1 Pork tenderloin

This is a good idea—just writing your list on a coupon. But the list doesn't seem to include eggs.

June 1st - June 15th

Hy-Vee Large Eggs
1 Dozen

Limit one coupon per customer.
Coupon valid from June 1st through June 15th, 2005

3/99¢

Limit 3

LU#1306

Hy-Vee
EMPLOYEE OWNED FOOD STORES

milk 1% + skim yogurt
white grape juice

Cream of celery soup
shredded cheddar cheese

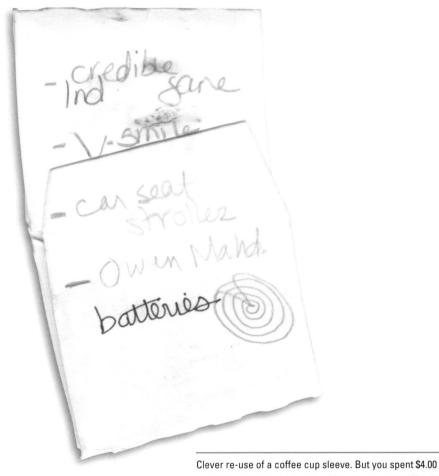

Clever re-use of a coffee cup sleeve. But you spent $4.00 on coffee and saved a fraction of a cent on paper. Nice job!

Otto Frederick Rohwedder has been called the Father of Sliced Bread. His early 20th century experiments resulted in a machine that could slice bread AND wrap it, which finally allowed the concept to catch on.

Apple pie was a popular breakfast in rural homes in the 19th century. Far from being a treat, it was considered a hearty beginning to a day full of hard work.

I bet your glove compartment is full of potential grocery list paper (i.e. unused fast food napkins).

Burgers
Ketchup
Cheese
Onion
tomato
chips

diet coke
breakfast

SPINACH
RED LEAF
Rabe
CABBAGE
cilantro
MINT
FLAT PARSLEY
carrot TOP
16 OZ Radish
cucumber
popJ·SL·CAB

celery
peas
cauliflower
MANGOS
Greens
MIN. EGGPLANT
EGGPLANT
cabbage
3 LB carrot
PICKLING

The corrugated cardboard grocery
list is the manliest way to shop.

94
CHAPTER 8

The favor of a reply was requested, but the card got used for a grocery list instead!

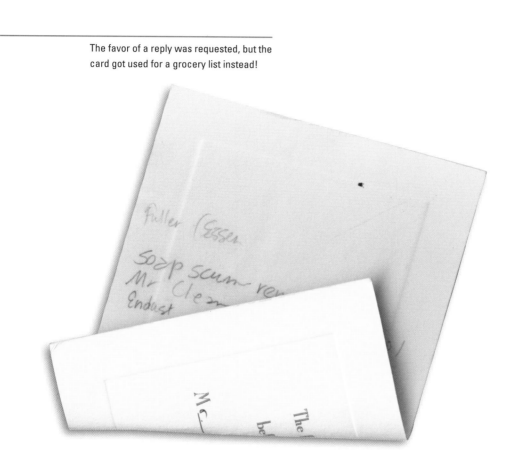

Amazingly, the average American eats 4.5 pounds of broccoli every year.
This is less than 20% of the amount of candy we consume annually.

And the award for "Worst Recycling Idea" goes to Nazia of
California. Congratulations Nazia, you've just won a lifetime
supply of identity theft!

Here's another bad idea: Using a bank deposit slip. With your name, address and phone on it. And, of course, your account number.

CHECKS LIST SINGLY	DOLLARS	CENTS
1		
2		
3		
4		
5		
6		
7		
8		
9		
10		
11		
12		
13		

milk

eggs

Bacon

toilet paper

2 lbs leeks

vermouth

lemons

garlic

parsley

green onions

Bermuda onion

2 lbs broccoli

basil

2 lbs new potatoes

dry white wine-cookin-

caraway seeds

Out of all the pens and scraps of paper lying around the house, you had to go and use a dark gray paint sample with black ink. What the hell is wrong with you?

Butter has been dyed yellow for at least 700 years. People used to use marigolds.

The best way to save time, money and paper seems to be to use the newspaper circular itself. Genius!

FINEST QUALITY MEAT

SALMON Eggs lasagna beef cheese noodles bacon dates

Dominick's
The Fresh Store

VALU
PACK
BUY BIG & SAVE

Cook
Internally to
160°F

Fresh 80% Lean
Ground Beef
Valu Pack.
Without card regular price
SAVE up to $1.30 lb.

1⁹⁹

Pork Shoulder
Blade Roast
Bone-in.
Government inspected.
Without card regular price
SAVE up to $1.70 lb.

99¢

Coffee

Beer

~~Oil~~

Chicken

3 ~~Bean Salad~~

~~Danish Rolls~~

99 ¢

CapitalOne

Total enclosed $

7

Capital One
P.O. Box 856
Richmond, VA

E/ 102 / 7708 / 7002 /COLLECT

Or, if you're the complete opposite of genius, use the back of your credit card's "payment enclosed" form, account number and all. Once again, smooth move, Donald!

9.

DOODLES
AND NOODLES

the art of the found grocery list

Not creatively satisfied with simply writing down "toilet paper, eggs, Pop-Tarts"—
some folks are compelled to doodle on their lists. Maybe it's just a scribble;
maybe it's a complete self-portrait. I haven't found any true masterpieces yet,
but y'all keep trying!

lettuce
cucumber
Red Salad onion   1
(leaves) -

2 - hamb   almond
                  flavor
green beans
wmelon
bananas
Cheeto balls

hyu - 2

Cheeto balls and a bucket of hooch—
two great tastes that taste great together.

Breakfast of champions? 12% of all soda sold in America is imbibed as—or with—breakfast.

Diet ~~~~~~~~
Sensodyne toothpaste
kid-chewi-vits
Fibre-all

pepperoni

Cheesestick~

This person always draws at least one of the items on her list. In this case, it's ginger, or a fat cat with a stubby tail, or a small pile of poop.

Carrots (big)
Red Peppers
Ginger

Granola Bars etc.
Pretzels
CANS BROTH:
BEEF + CHICKEN

Bear Tea
CAT LITTER + LINERS
SELTZER

Sandwich bags
Tin Foil

Yeah, this is the only sexy grocery list I've ever seen. *Hello!*

They say all children are artists, but I beg to differ.

coffee
sugar
creamer
mayo
bubbles
tape
lollipop
butter
syrup
toothpaste

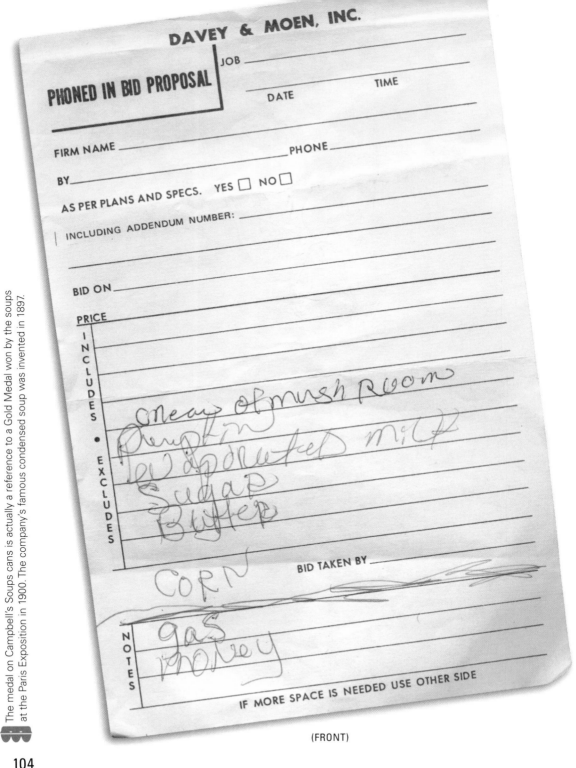

DAVEY & MOEN, INC.

PHONED IN BID PROPOSAL

JOB _____

DATE _____ TIME _____

FIRM NAME _____ PHONE _____

BY _____

AS PER PLANS AND SPECS.   YES ☐   NO ☐

INCLUDING ADDENDUM NUMBER: _____

_____

BID ON _____

PRICE _____

INCLUDES

EXCLUDES

Cream of mushroom
pumpkin
evaporated milk
sugar
butter

CORN

BID TAKEN BY _____

NOTES

gas
money

IF MORE SPACE IS NEEDED USE OTHER SIDE

(FRONT)

The medal on Campbell's Soups cans is actually a reference to a Gold Medal won by the soups at the Paris Exposition in 1900. The company's famous condensed soup was invented in 1897.

General Foods chemists invented a way to put carbon dioxide in a solid back in the 1950s. They didn't figure out how to take advantage of the process until the company started marketing Pop Rocks in the 1970s.

"Attention shoppers: Demon in aisle five. Demon in aisle five."

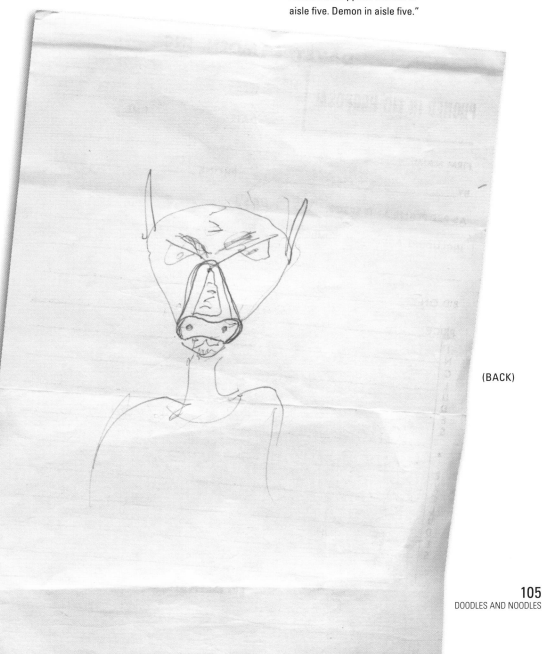

(BACK)

hummus - bread

Bananas - Apples etc ORANGES

Lettuce (5)

Carrots big + l'il

Red Peppers

Cukes

Celery

Broccoli

De-caf Coffee ((Vanilla?)

PASTA shapes

CAN of Tuna

Deli stubb

V-8 cans
juice oxs

Seltzer
★ Cans of Soup

Yogurt
Eggs half + half
milk
Cheese-stix
FRZN:
Veg. All kinds

baem?

Look, up in the sky! It's Supershopperwoman and her amazing cans of soup.

In 1900 Hershey's invented its famous milk chocolate bar. Reese's Peanut Butter Cups and Butterfinger bars date to 1923. Snickers came around in 1930 and Kit Kat in 1933. M&M's were invented in 1940.

The original Three Musketeers candy bars actually included three different bars in one package, each with their own flavor.

"I'm watching you shop!"

"I want this type of spring chicken ... the kind that looks like batteries."

EGGS   Gummi Vitamins
+EGG WHITE   COCOA
MILK   CHEESE STICKS
[Dish Soap]

Dhanya
Aloo
Spring onion ② or ③
French beans.
Peas.
evaporated Can.
chicken.
Fresh Cream. 2 tbsp.

"Please get a peeler when you go to the store. It looks like this."

Canned hams: First sold by Hormel in 1926.

~~Garlic~~
mushrooms!

peeler ↗ ! ! !
big carrots
Potatoes
Baking Apples
Quick Oats
Cheese + Crackers?
Nuts?
Cider   eggs!
Bathroom Spray

Salad stuff
Fruit

Diet Cocoa

Lite Olive

Spray Olive oil
w canola

Rice-cakes
Box broth
peeler →

Eggs
Milk
STAMPS!

eye
stuff ←

"I said, please get a peeler
when you go to the store.
It looks like this."

10.

JUST ONE THING

extremely short shopping lists

Some lists are so short you wonder why anyone even bothered to write down one or two items in the first place. Of course, I understand these lists function more as a reminder than a shopping list. We're all so overwhelmed with information and things to do that it's easy to forget the milk on the way home from work.

But what I find funny is that people will make that short list, go to the store, carry the list into the store, find the one thing they want, and then leave the list in the cart. They were only buying one thing! Yet not only did they need to reference the list—they used a cart to haul that one item to the checkout! Ha! Funny, right? Oh, America, you amuse me.

Yeah. So. You decided to
have spaghetti for dinner.
DID YOU REALLY NEED TO
MAKE A LIST?

Spaghetti
Spaghetti Sauce
Garlic Bread

LOEWS
BEVERLY HILLS HOTEL
LOS ANGELES

Water
heetergent

Tel (310) 277-2800 Fax (310) 203-9537

I hate doing the laundry
too, but at least I don't need
to be reminded of the two
main ingredients. Of course,
if you're from Beverly Hills,
maybe you've never done the
laundry yourself before.

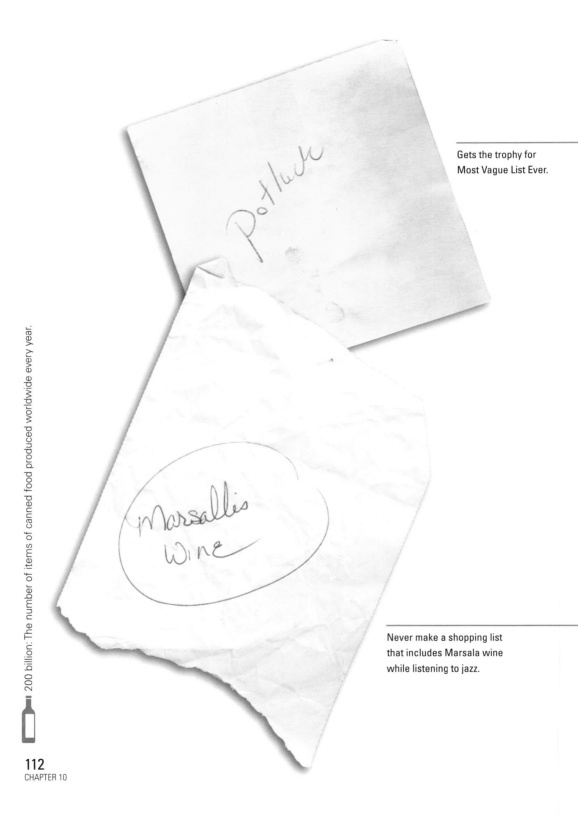

Gets the trophy for
Most Vague List Ever.

Never make a shopping list
that includes Marsala wine
while listening to jazz.

200 billion: The number of items of canned food produced worldwide every year.

Mozzarella
pizza sauce

beer

Would have been a perfect evening had
they remembered "dough" and "porno."

cheese
crackers

Forgetful person in
the mood for a snack.

Va-va-voom! Now we're talking!

Salt, milk and a stupid
little notepad.

The cash register was invented by James Ritty, of Dayton, Ohio, in order to prevent employee theft.

SHOPPING FOR TROUBLE

Retail manager Don ("Just Don") has found many discarded shopping lists in his Maryland market over the years, but this one is special. It's more than just a short, strange shopping list—it's a shopLIFTing list.

As Don posted to his weblog: "What is interesting about these shopping lists are that they are always dropped by a serial shoplifter on his way out of the store. The items on his lists are what he steals. So he is planning his thefts ahead of time."

Another strange fact about this fellow, an elderly gentleman dubbed "The Cigarette/DVD Guy," is that he scrawls these shoplifting lists on the back of business cards. Don doesn't know if the person on the card is the shoplifter, but he's anticipating Cigarette/DVD Guy's next visit: "If he ever does return I'm stopping him and banning him from the store. I am actually looking forward to him showing up again since I keep one of his dropped cards in my wallet at all times. If and when I see him again, I'm going to call the number that is on the face of the business card and see if the cell phone on his belt rings."

Don imagines the following conversation might ensue...

Don: "Hey ... yeah. Is this [name redacted]? How are you doing today?"

Shoplifter: "Uhhh ... I'm fine. Who is this?"

Don: "The store manager. Right behind you." Waves and smiles. "Get out of the store and don't return, please. Thanks."

*Fike wood
Tylonal
Pm.*

About 2% of adults and 8% of children have a food allergy.

The least healthy breakfast I have ever seen.

No doubt purchased in order to attach grocery lists to forehead.

Suction Cups

Adhesive clips

celery

If I were going to make a list with just one thing on it, this wouldn't be it.

It's ironic that green tea is supposed to be good for your memory, isn't it?

Green Tea!

Seems like the longest possible way to say "hot dogs." Six words for one item!

Original Reg
All Beef Kosha
Natural

Tomato ketchup debuted around the end of the 18th century.

That 12 oz. aluminum can you're drinking from? Royal Crown Cola introduced it in 1964. Coca-Cola took another three years to get on board.

Cat litter
salads

Blecchhhhhh!

noodles
sauce

OK, Einstein.

It's taco night at the old folks home. I love taco night.

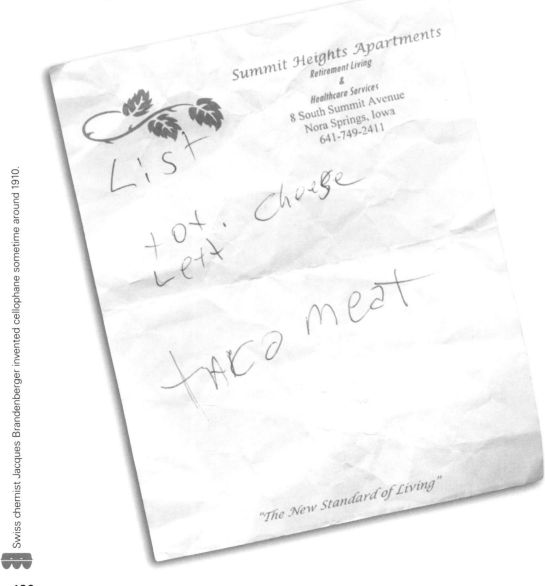

Summit Heights Apartments
Retirement Living
&
Healthcare Services
8 South Summit Avenue
Nora Springs, Iowa
641-749-2411

List
tot. Cheese
Lett.

taco meat

"The New Standard of Living"

Dairy. Snot rags. Done.

½ gallon whole
Milk

1 Half & Half

2 Kleenex

DESITIN
CREAMY

...ligating, but you are still obligated to pay the...parts of your
...tion, we cannot report you as delinquent or take any action to

...you purchased with a credit card, and you have tried in good
...to pay the remaining amount due on the goods or services. You
...50 and the purchase was made in your home state... within 100
...or if we mailed you the... ...for the property or
...on of purchase.

...age daily balance we take the beginning balance of your account
...its and unpaid finance charges. This gives us a daily balance.
...de the total by the number of days in the billing cycle. This is your
...the date of each advance.

...erned by any agreement between us and/or all applicable rules
...the National Automated Clearing House Association (NACHA
...ement is wrong, please telephone us at the number listed on the

U.S. Bank Member FDIC

Because "Desitin Crunchy" would
be wrong in so many ways. Well,
just one way, but you get my point.

Zest is the colored outermost skin layer of citrus fruits. Zest is highly perfumed and is rich in flavonoids, bioflavonoids, and limonoids.

You needed a list for the two most clichéd grocery store items in the entire history of the universe?

Trader
Joe's   Bread
sk. milk

Half and Half
✗

Straight-Edge caffeine freak?

11.

YOU'RE SO VAGUE

"supper, dinner, food, stuff..."

Whenever I find a list that has "supper" or "dinner" or "food" written on it, I picture the meals from *The Simpsons*. As if "dinner" was a blobby monochromatic product that comes in a plain box stamped "Dinner."

Dinner—or Powerade? Tough choice.

Wisconsin's 1.3 million dairy cows produce a year's supply of milk for nearly 42 million people, butter for 68 million, and cheese for 86 million.

OVBC
Jeannie's
Degree

body wash
shampoo
buns
lunch meat
supper

The only thing missing seems
to be "breakfast food."

- Alum Foil
- milk ①
- Bread
  - meals?

www.hawkeyeautobody.com

HAWKEYE
AUTO BODY

2111 S. Federal Ave. Mason City, IA 50401
Phone: 641-424-4973 Fax: 641-424-3198

Meals? Yes, maybe you
should get some meals.

dog food
drájno
bread
peanut butter
grapes
oranges
diet coke
dinners

"Dinners." Yummy, delicious dinners.

Shopping List

@ lunch
@ snacks

dent.
lunch/
dinner

Well, you gotta have
priorities. Snacks will
probably beat out salad
and lunch every time.

Kiwifruits have more than twice the vitamin C of oranges, as much potassium as bananas, and are a good source of magnesium, fiber and vitamin E. They have only 45 calories each.

If you run out of confectioner's sugar, you can make a good substitute by putting some regular sugar in a blender with a pinch of cornstarch.

So I guess that means the hot dogs are for dinner.

deodorant
milk
oj
ice cream
lunch stuff
hot dogs

4 LUNCHES
2 LUNCHES
7 FRUIT
WATER
CEREAL
CREAM WHETT
FRUITCUPS
BREAD

1 MILK
1 MILK

NOSE BREATHE
TOOTHPASTE

Make up your mind! Do you want
four lunches or two lunches?

Who cares about "supper" when you can have "buster?"

-bread
- Milk
-Juice
-chips
-yogurt
-lunchmeat
-Buster
-Supper

STURDY REMINDER:
GROCERY LIST DECOUPAGE TABLE

A couple years ago I got an e-mail from a grocerylists.org reader named Rose McKee, who was working in a grocery store in Austin, Texas. Admitting that she was the forgetful type, she decided to decoupage a kitchen table with grocery lists she had found discarded at the store. The idea being that before she went shopping she would sit at the table to make her list and have a handy suggestion guide right in front of her. Much better than going shopping for "lunch stuff" or "dinner." Yay for Rose!

"Mexican or Southern dinner"—
because they're so similar.

lettuce
tomato
roast beef
turkey
~~cheese~~,
thomas'
sesame bagels
k sandwich bread
nail polish remover

mexican or southern
dinner
toast bread
fresh fruit

131
YOU'RE SO VAGUE

Montpelier, Vermont, is the only U.S. state capital without a McDonald's restaurant.

Supper? What is this thing you call supper? I will have cheese instead.

milk
ketchup
paper cups
~~*supper*~~ *?*
cheese

Some supper for the bird, and some supper for me.

wh. wh. bread
bird seed
Klondikes
SUPPER

Ahem, just don't eat that dinner before your colon checkup. (Fleet Bowel Prep. is a product for patients about to undergo endoscopy.)

Fruit, dinner, weed killer.

Vernor's Ginger Ale was the first soda pop made in the U.S. It was created in Detroit, Michigan, in 1866 by James Vernor. He sold it in his drug store for thirty years before opening a factory.

"Supper food."

Dog Food
Cereal
Snacks
Supper Food
Soda.

Water Bill
Phone Bill
Muffin Mix
    choc chip
    Bl. Berry

Gabriel Garcia Marquez
"Love in the time of
Cholera"

These internal adament 'screams'; tug at my gut. I am nauseated. I want to throw-up on my congested black honey on these criyed-face biting-wasp.

Joseph is a big blue elephant

In 1939 the seedless watermelon was developed by treating the unpollinated flowers of watermelons with a type of acid.

At first you think the list is odd because the only food item on it is, well, "food." Then you read the rest: "These internal adament (sic) 'screams' tug at my gut. I am nauseated. I want to throw up my congested black honey on these criyed-face biting-wasp (sic)." Also, "Joseph is a big blue elephant."

12.

ORGANIZED LISTS
O.C.D. at the S.T.O.R.E.

Grocery shopping must be pure joy for the obsessive-compulsive. Aisle after aisle of precisely arranged products grouped into categories and neatly stacked on clean shelves. Some uber-organized shoppers sort their lists by aisle. Others use a pre-formatted master list so they can just check off the things they need without having to write much down. Strangely, efficiency and laziness actually go quite well together, like pickles and peanut butter.

The ultimate basic grocery shopping organizational tool: A pre-planned list that includes quantities, specific products and price points, printed onto an envelope that holds your coupons. Simple, but very effective.

Carrot, broc, onion
Creamer
Milk
Nesquik (4)
Insoles
Glade spray (2)
Cheese (string, pjack, ched)
Yoplait (6)
Freezer ziplocs
Coke
Chips
Evap milk
Pasta (5)
Campbells Select (3)
Beef broth
Garbanzo beans
Sara lee buns
Hot pockets ($1.50)
Halloween candy

Margarine was developed in 1869 by Hippolyte Mège-Mouriés, a French chemist. Napoleon III had offered a prize for a butter substitute for his army and navy, because butter spoiled easily.

"I'm very organized. I clip the coupons to my list so I don't forget to give them to the cashier." Oops.

S
fish
bread
lemon
broccoli

M
pork chops
white rice
(cauliflower)

T
sausage
lettuce

W
risotto stir
fry

TH
frozen food
fruit
organic PB

Yogurt

string beans
1 pack salami
rolls
oran juice

The shopping list as weekly menu planner. Nice!

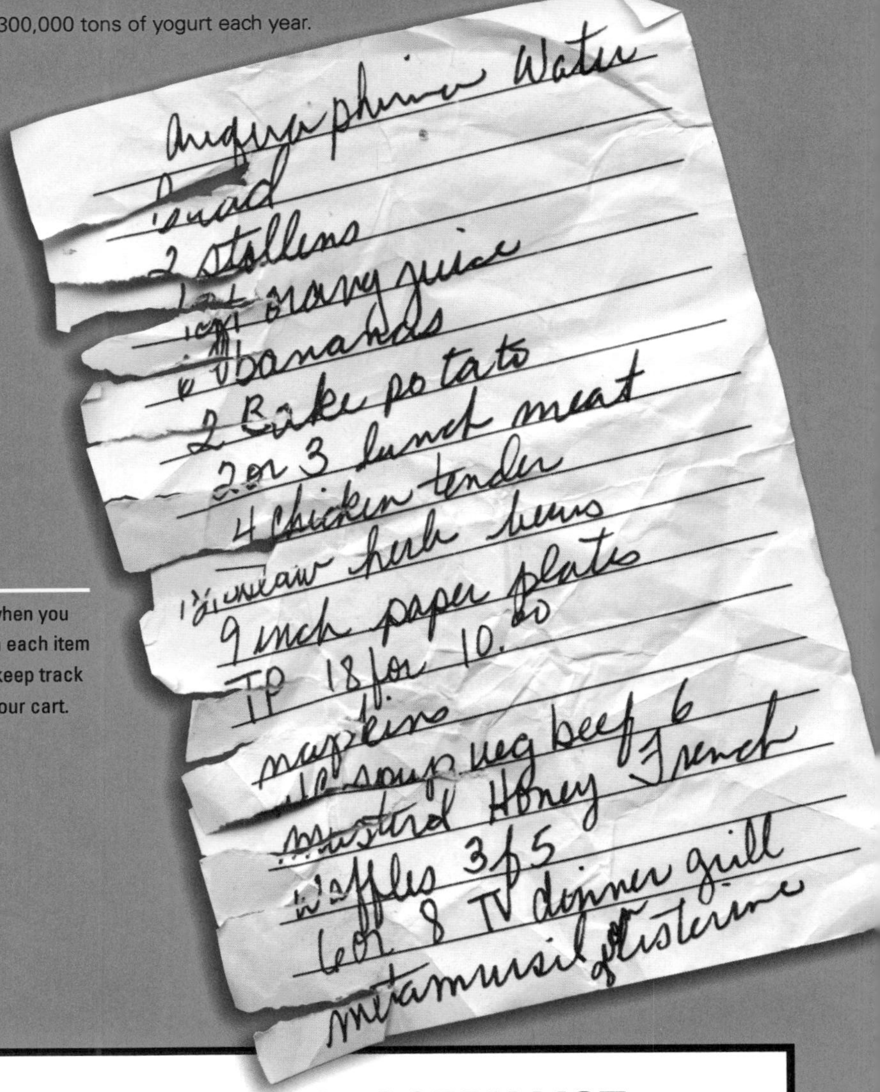

If you forget a writing utensil when you go to the store, tearing through each item as you pick it up can help you keep track of what you've already got in your cart.

[Handwritten grocery list:]

Angiyaphina Water
bread
2 stollins
cranberry juice
bananas
2 Bake potato
2 or 3 lunch meat
4 chicken tender
brazilian herb beans
9 inch paper plates
TP 18 for 10.00
napkins
soup veg beef 6
mustard Honey French
Waffles 3 f 5
6 or 8 TV dinner grill
miamusil glisterine

THE ULTIMATEST GROCERY LIST

I made this grocery list just for you. It's the best grocery list ever made. You will find that your shopping experience is much more satisfying when you go to the store organized and prepared. You can either photocopy the next page or go to www.grocerylists.org to download the file as a printable PDF. Enjoy!

Developed by Rudolph Boysen in the early 1930s, the boysenberry is a cross between a loganberry, red raspberry and blackberry.

The Ultimatest Grocery List | www.grocerylists.org

Fresh vegetables
- ○ Asparagus
- ○ Beets
- ○ Broccoli / Cauliflower
- ○ Carrots
- ○ Celery
- ○ Corn
- ○ Cucumbers
- ○ Greens
- ○ Lettuce
- ○ Mushrooms
- ○ Onions
- ○ Peppers
- ○ Potatoes
- ○ Spinach
- ○ Sprouts
- ○ Squash
- ○ Tomatoes
- ○ Zucchini
- ○ Other_____
- ○ Other_____

Fresh fruits
- ○ Apples
- ○ Avocado
- ○ Bananas
- ○ Berries
- ○ Cherries
- ○ Grapes
- ○ Kiwis
- ○ Lemons / Limes
- ○ Melons
- ○ Oranges
- ○ Peaches
- ○ Pears
- ○ Plums
- ○ Other_____
- ○ Other_____

Canned foods
- ○ Applesauce
- ○ Baked beans
- ○ Beans
- ○ Carrots
- ○ Corn
- ○ Beans
- ○ Mixed fruit
- ○ Mixed veggies
- ○ Olives
- ○ Pasta sauce
- ○ Pickles
- ○ Refried beans
- ○ Tuna
- ○ Soups
- ○ Tomatoes
- ○ Other_____
- ○ Other_____

Sauces
- ○ BBQ sauce
- ○ Hot sauce
- ○ Salsa
- ○ Soy sauce
- ○ Steak sauce
- ○ Syrup
- ○ Worcestershire sauce
- ○ Other_____
- ○ Other_____

Various groceries
- ○ Bottled water
- ○ Bullion cubes
- ○ Cereal
- ○ Coffee
- ○ Gravy
- ○ Honey
- ○ Jelly / Preserves
- ○ Ketchup
- ○ Lemon / Lime juice
- ○ Mac & cheese
- ○ Mayonnaise
- ○ Mustard
- ○ Pancake / Waffle mix
- ○ Peanut butter
- ○ Ramen
- ○ Soda pop
- ○ Tea
- ○ White rice
- ○ Wild rice
- ○ Other_____
- ○ Other_____

Spices & herbs
- ○ Basil
- ○ Black pepper
- ○ Cilantro
- ○ Cinnamon
- ○ Garlic
- ○ Oregano
- ○ Parsley
- ○ Red pepper
- ○ Salt
- ○ Vanilla extract
- ○ Other_____
- ○ Other_____

Oils/Vinegars
- ○ Apple cider vinegar
- ○ Balsamic vinegar
- ○ Salad dressing
- ○ Olive oil
- ○ Vegetable oil
- ○ White vinegar
- ○ Other_____
- ○ Other_____

Refrigerated items
- ○ Chip dip
- ○ Eggs / Fake eggs
- ○ Juice
- ○ Ready-bake breads
- ○ Tofu
- ○ Tortillas
- ○ Other_____
- ○ Other_____

Dairy
- ○ Butter
- ○ Half & half
- ○ Heavy cream
- ○ Margarine
- ○ Milk
- ○ Sour cream
- ○ Whipped cream
- ○ Yogurt
- ○ Other_____
- ○ Other_____

Cheese
- ○ Cheddar
- ○ Cottage cheese
- ○ Cream cheese
- ○ Feta
- ○ Mozzarella
- ○ Parmesan
- ○ Pepper
- ○ Provolone
- ○ Ricotta
- ○ Sandwich slices
- ○ Shredded
- ○ Swiss
- ○ Other_____
- ○ Other_____

Frozen
- ○ Burittos
- ○ Desserts
- ○ Fish sticks
- ○ Ice cream
- ○ Juices
- ○ Pizzas
- ○ Popsicles
- ○ Fries / Tater tots
- ○ Sorbet
- ○ TV dinners
- ○ Vegetables
- ○ Veggie burgers
- ○ Other_____
- ○ Other_____

Meat
- ○ Bacon
- ○ Beef
- ○ Chicken
- ○ Ground beef
- ○ Ground turkey
- ○ Ham
- ○ Hot dogs
- ○ Lunchmeat
- ○ Pork
- ○ Sausage
- ○ Steak
- ○ Turkey
- ○ Other_____
- ○ Other_____

Seafood
- ○ Catfish
- ○ Cocktail sauce
- ○ Crab
- ○ Halibut
- ○ Oysters
- ○ Salmon
- ○ Shrimp
- ○ Tilapia
- ○ Tuna
- ○ Other_____
- ○ Other_____

Baked goods
- ○ Bagels
- ○ Buns
- ○ Cake
- ○ Cookies
- ○ Crackers
- ○ Croissants

(column)
- ○ Donuts
- ○ Fresh bread
- ○ Pastries
- ○ Pie
- ○ Pitas
- ○ Rolls
- ○ Sliced bread
- ○ Other_____
- ○ Other_____

Baking
- ○ Baking powder
- ○ Baking soda
- ○ Bread crumbs
- ○ Brown sugar
- ○ Cake decorations
- ○ Cake icing
- ○ Cake / Brownie mix
- ○ Chocolate chips
- ○ Cocoa
- ○ Flour
- ○ Oatmeal
- ○ Pie shell
- ○ Powdered sugar
- ○ Shortening
- ○ Sugar
- ○ Yeast
- ○ Other_____
- ○ Other_____

Snacks
- ○ Candy
- ○ Cookies
- ○ Dried fruit
- ○ Granola bars
- ○ Gum
- ○ Nuts
- ○ Popcorn
- ○ Potato chips
- ○ Pudding
- ○ Pretzels
- ○ Tortilla chips
- ○ Other_____
- ○ Other_____

Personal care
- ○ Antiperspirant
- ○ Bath soap
- ○ Conditioner
- ○ Condoms
- ○ Cosmetics
- ○ Deodorant
- ○ Facial cleanser
- ○ Facial tissue
- ○ Floss
- ○ Hair gel/spray
- ○ Hand soap
- ○ Lip balm
- ○ Moisturizing lotion
- ○ Mouthwash
- ○ Q-Tips
- ○ Razors
- ○ Shampoo
- ○ Shaving cream
- ○ Toilet paper
- ○ Toothpaste
- ○ Other_____
- ○ Other_____

Medicine
- ○ Allergy
- ○ Antidiarrheal
- ○ Aspirin
- ○ Antacid
- ○ Band-aids
- ○ Cold
- ○ Feminine products
- ○ Prescription
- ○ Sinus
- ○ Vitamins
- ○ Other_____
- ○ Other_____

Kitchen
- ○ Aluminum foil
- ○ Coffee filters
- ○ Dish soap
- ○ Dishwasher soap
- ○ Disposable cups
- ○ Disposable cutlery
- ○ Disposable plates
- ○ Freezer bags
- ○ Napkins
- ○ Non-stick spray
- ○ Paper towels
- ○ Plastic wrap
- ○ Roasting pan
- ○ Sandwich bags
- ○ Sponges / Scrubbers
- ○ Wax paper
- ○ Other_____
- ○ Other_____

Cleaning products
- ○ Air freshener
- ○ Bathroom cleaner
- ○ Bleach
- ○ Dryer sheets
- ○ Fabric softener
- ○ Floor cleaner
- ○ Garbage bags
- ○ Glass cleaner
- ○ Laundry detergent
- ○ Mop head
- ○ Spray polish
- ○ Vacuum bags
- ○ Other_____
- ○ Other_____

Other stuff
- ○ Automotive
- ○ Batteries
- ○ Candles
- ○ CDRs
- ○ Charcoal
- ○ Fresh flowers
- ○ Greeting cards
- ○ Hardware
- ○ Insect repellent
- ○ Insecticides
- ○ Light bulbs
- ○ Magazine
- ○ Newspaper
- ○ Random impulse buy
- ○ Sunscreen
- ○ Other_____
- ○ Other_____

Pets
- ○ Cat food
- ○ Cat litter
- ○ Cat treats
- ○ Dog food
- ○ Dog treats
- ○ Flea treatment
- ○ Pet shampoo
- ○ Other_____
- ○ Other_____

Baby
- ○ Baby food
- ○ Bottles / Cups
- ○ Diapers
- ○ Diaper lotion
- ○ Formula
- ○ Wipes
- ○ Other_____
- ○ Other_____

Office supplies
- ○ Envelopes
- ○ Glue
- ○ Notepads
- ○ Paper
- ○ Pens / Pencils
- ○ Scotch tape
- ○ Other_____
- ○ Other_____

Alcohol
- ○ Beer
- ○ Champagne
- ○ Club soda
- ○ Gin
- ○ Malt beverage
- ○ Red wine
- ○ Rum
- ○ Sake
- ○ Tonic
- ○ Whiskey
- ○ White wine
- ○ Vodka
- ○ Other_____
- ○ Other_____

Themed meals
- ○ Burger night
- ○ Chili night
- ○ Pizza night
- ○ Spaghetti night
- ○ Taco night
- ○ Take-out deli food
- ○ Other_____
- ○ Other_____

Other
- ○ _____
- ○ _____
- ○ _____
- ○ _____
- ○ _____
- ○ _____
- ○ _____
- ○ _____

IMPORTANT: Please leave this list in the cart when you're done.

If found, please mail to Grocerylists.org, P.O. Box 752, St. Louis, MO 63188 USA

Grocerylists.org is the world's largest online collection of found grocery lists. Visit our shopping blog, our hilarious Top 10 lists, learn about our book of shopping lists or just waste time browsing the thousands of discarded lists in the collection: **www.grocerylists.org**.

THE ULTIMATEST GROCERY LIST, THE DELUXE VERSION ©2007 GROCERYLISTS.ORG

Before you go
- ○ Bring canvas bags
- ○ Clip coupons
- ○ Film to process?
- ○ Plastic bags to recycle?
- ○ Return anything?

Before you check out
- ○ Need ice?
- ○ Rent movie
- ○ Pick up photos
- ○ Stock on sale items
- ○ Use your coupons!

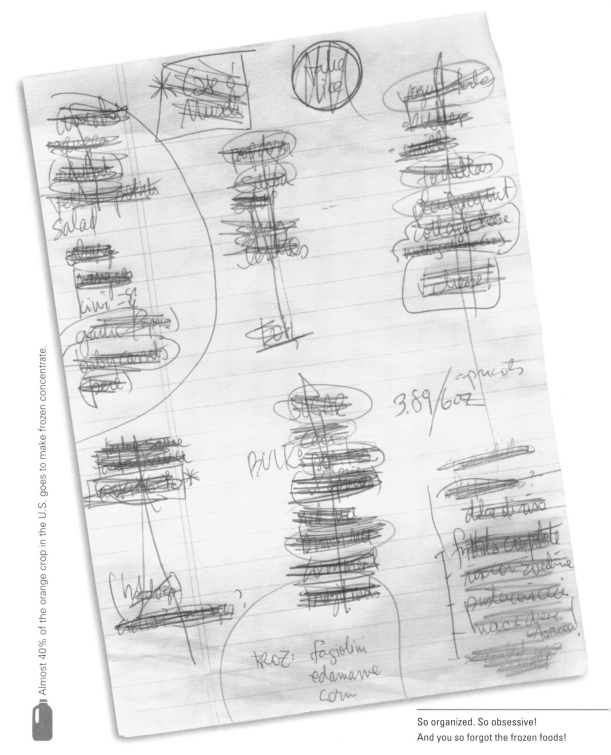

So organized. So obsessive!
And you so forgot the frozen foods!

Sometimes even the simplest things need to be written down. Like the names of family members, and your favorite brands of yucky beers.

Fish Dinner
1. Dad
2. Danny
3. Mom
4. Kathy
5. Tracey
6. Kevin
    Girls

Beer
- Bud Light /Mickeys
° Pop
° Plastic Cups

In 1995 Nabisco produced 16 billion Oreo cookies at its factory in Chicago, Illinois, the largest of its kind in the world.

Who'd have though that squiggly lines would ADD order to a grocery list?

Vidalia onions, by law, can only be grown in twenty Georgia counties.

Olive trees may live to be 1,500 years old; the average life span is about 500 years.

1. Car #1
   Whole Foods
   ↳ cereal
   ↳ tea
   ↳ Cranberry juice
   ↳ water bottles
2. Car #2
   Wal Mart
   ↳ ~~say much~~
   ↳ ~~pills~~
   ↳ ~~popsicles~~
   ↳ flashlight / candle
   ↳ ~~water bottles~~

They're so organized they've dispatched Car No. 1 and Car No. 2 out on shopping trips. But both of them are coming back with water bottles.

One way to be sure you buy the right kind of ribbon is to snip a piece and staple it to your shopping list. Another way is to ... well, I guess there is no other way.

The shopping cart is called a "buggy" or "trolley" in the U.K.

146
CHAPTER 12

Chesapeake Bay oyster production in the late 19th century was over 111 million pounds; in 1980 it was 22 million pounds; in 1990 it was less than 4 million pounds.

3 1/2 cups Spelt flour
2 tablespoons Sunflower seeds
2 tablespoons Sesame seeds
1 tablespoon Flax seeds
1 Tablespoon pumpkin seeds
2 1/2 Tablespoons cracked rye
2 1/2 Tablespoons cracked wheat
1/3 cup Spelt/wheat flakes
1/3 cup toasted walnut halves, chopped
1/2 cup toasted almonds, coarsley chopped
1/3 cup toasted hazelnuts.

I suppose one way to make sure you don't forget anything for the recipe is to bring the recipe to the store.

Tea bags were first used commercially in 1904. Thomas Sullivan of New York first used them to send samples to his customers instead of sealing the tea in more expensive tins.

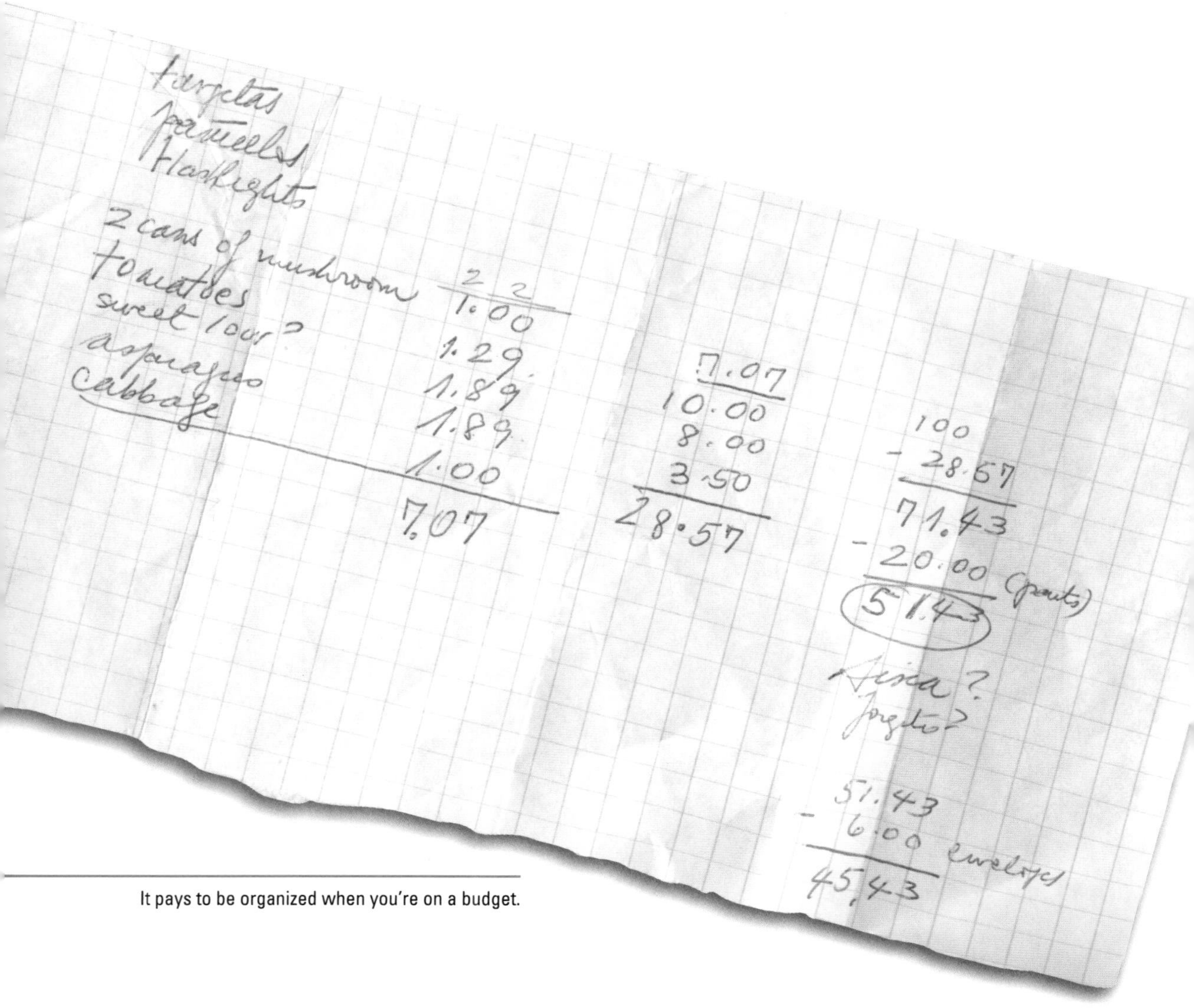

(handwritten note on graph paper)

tarjetas
pañuelos
Flashlights

2 cans of mushroom   2   2
tomatoes   1.00
sweet corn?   1.29
asparagus   1.89
cabbage   1.89
   1.00
   7.07

7.07
10.00
8.00
3.50
28.57

100
− 28.57
71.43
− 20.00 (pants)
51.43

Aixa?
Jorgito?

51.43
− 6.00 envelopes
45.43

It pays to be organized when you're on a budget.

13.

YE OLDE STYLE

the lists of the elderly

There's more than one way to spot an elderly person. It's not just that they look, well, old. It's their grocery lists. The lists of the elderly are almost always written in shaky capital letters. They almost always include prices; only old people have enough time to read every grocery store ad in the newspaper, then compare them. And they all include sweets. Because at that age, the last thing you're worrying about is your teeth. I think when you get old enough you forget what teeth are, until you see nice ones, which just makes you grumpy. Anyway. When I'm old, this will be my grocery list, every day: corn dogs, pizza rolls, whole milk, steak, Whatchamacallit candy bars, moisturizing lotion, Southern Comfort, Lucky Strikes (filters).

Unfortunately, I won't live to be very old, because that really is my grocery list (minus the Lucky Strikes, which I can't wait to start smoking again when I get old).

Old people like cookies.

Malt-O-Meal, prune juice, a vanity stool, hemorrhoidal suppositories. Old person!

In 1903, James L. Kraft, with a rented cart and $65 in capital, began a wholesale cheese business in Chicago. The company introduced Cheez Whiz in 1952.

Honestly, the only thing written on this list that I can decipher is "fish eye," and I don't know what the hell that means.

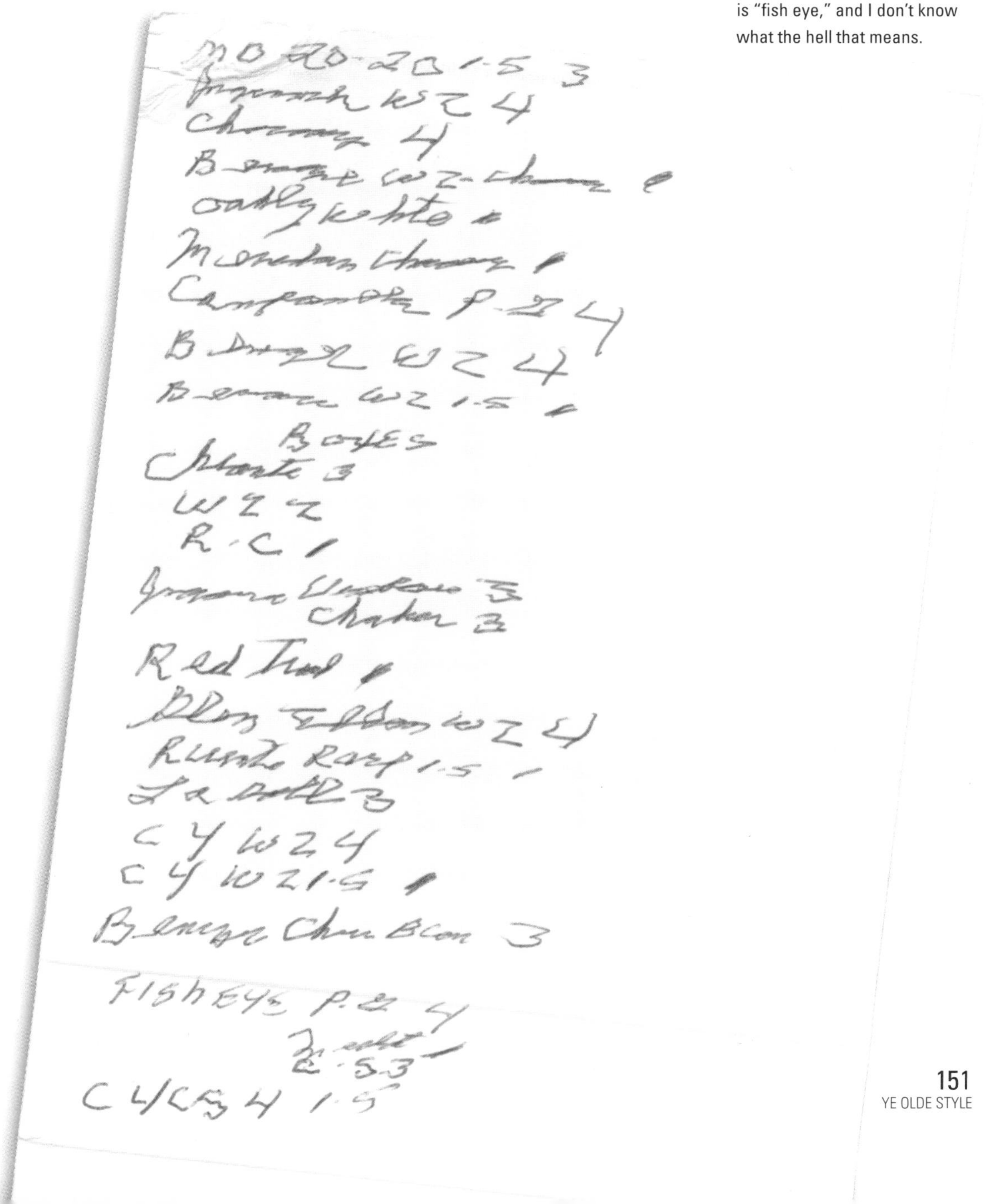

A SHORT HISTORY OF GROCERY LISTS

Speaking of old things, some of the oldest surviving grocery lists are in the collection of The British Museum. They are part of a large set of ancient documents called the Vindolanda writing tablets, excavated from the Roman fort at Vindolanda in Northern England, just south of Hadrian's Wall. The lists, found in 1973 with a great number of other Latin documents in a soggy trash pile, date to the 1st century A.D. A few of the postcard-sized pieces of wood can be considered grocery lists. Vindolanda Tablet 203, Leaf No. 1 (shown below) has been translated as: "… bruised beans, two modii, chickens, twenty, a hundred apples, if you can find nice ones, a hundred or two hundred eggs, if they are for sale there at a fair price. … 8 sextarii of fish-sauce … a modius of olives …" As I mentioned before, that sounds pretty familiar (aside from the Latin) despite the passage of two millennia.

My collection contains nothing so historically significant. I have a list from Pennsylvania from 1974. And I have the notepad of a woman who catalogued every penny she spent or received, including foodstuffs, carfare and room and board, for the year 1905. But nothing really impressive—like the 1465 grocery list of George Neville, Archbishop of York. When he was installed he held a feast, and what a feast it was. According to a 2005 *New York Times* book review of *Charlemagne's Tablecloth* by Nichola Fletcher, Neville's list called for "1,000 sheep, 7,000 capons, 1,000 egrets, 400 peacocks and 103 cold venison pasties. In all, 42,833 items of meat and poultry were served …"

© The British Museum

Female asparagus stalks are plumper than male stalks.

FRIDAY
4
JAN. 1974

DEC. 1973
S M T W T F S
1
2 3 4 5 6 7 8
9 10 11 12 13 14 15
16 17 18 19 20 21 22
23 24 25 26 27 28 29
30 31

FEB. 1974
S M T W T F S
1 2
3 4 5 6 7 8 9
10 11 12 13 14 15 16
17 18 19 20 21 22 23
24 25 26 27 28

– APPOINTMENTS –

8:00	sherbert
8:30	Wet ones
9:00	
9:30	Mandarin
10:00	
10:30	
11:00	
11:30	
12:00	
1:00	
1:30	
2:00	
2:30	Room fresh
3:00	
3:30	bread
4:00	
4:30	Rolls
5:00	lean Steak
5:30	w/mushrooms

MELLIN'S FOOD COMPANY
OF NORTH AMERICA
291 Atlantic Ave., Boston, Massachusetts
A duplicate pad for this cover will be sent on
application to Mellin's Food Company.

USE FRESH COW'S MILK
With MELLIN'S FOOD

Feb. 18 1905
paid board
pins   2.00
stamps   .15 —
thille   .15 —
cushion   .10
car fare   .18
Feb 21st   .25
rubbers
car fare   .60
baars rings   .20
Feb 23.   .30
car fare
lunch   .10
              .18

Dental tape. Nice handwriting for an old person, though.

Twinkies snack cakes were invented in 1930 by James Dewar, of the Continental Baking Company in Chicago.

Cho SURP
Ice CREAM
Sleep Aid
@ 99S
SOAP

Old people like ice cream.

CAKES
CHIPS
TOWEL
PA BEANS
SAUSAGE
T.V.
MILK
BREAD
ROLLS

Old people like cakes.

I think old people like ham, too.

Ham
Listerine
T paper

Potassium 99 m.g.
Super Earth Formulas
Multivitamin multim...
Suplement
Vitamin C
Mega Tabs
Zantac   Hernia
medigine
Ostee Bi Flex — for arthritis
Zero Dolphins

Tomato juice is the official state beverage of Ohio.

Old people like all sorts of medicines.

"Back in my day, we didn't have ditto marks. We had to write mushroom soup twice! And we liked it."

Bread
milk
Peaches
Mushroom Soup
"
"

Hominy
P. Towel
eggs
orange juice

Pills

And, of course, old people just LOVE pills in general.

14.

PLANET OF FOOD

grocery lists with a worldly flair

It's no surprise that the human diet has adapted and expanded over the years based on what's available (and moderately yummy). And despite the fact that centuries of world travel and decades of mass-production have spread processed and preserved foods across the globe, modern local cultures retain a certain amount of uniqueness. For example, I live in St. Louis, where it's not uncommon to find a grocery list featuring "toasted ravioli." But I've never seen a list from Australia that features that unlikely Midwestern specialty. Of course, I have yet to find a list in St. Louis that includes "Vegemite," like those from Down Under. And while St. Louis loves us some "gooey butter cake," "tinapay" is the more popular pastry in the Philippines. Just remember that even though the U.S. Senate doesn't want Americans to recite the Pledge of Allegiance in a foreign tongue, it can't stop you from shopping in Spanish. Or Arabic. Or Polish. Let's take a quick trip around the world and peek in on the planet's pantry.

Poo -
2 Tomatos -
1 piña abacada -
Apple Juice -
[crossed out]
1 caixa de ovos
Leg Ham - 200 gr
Butter Mentol -

This list was found in Australia: Oh. My. God.
They eat "poo" Down Under!

In Spanish (found in Chicago): Fried fish, garbanzo beans, roasted meat, back, garbanzo beans, tomato paste, laurel, meat, eggs, yogurt, olive, cheese, Swiffer, sponges, washing machine soap, apples, pears, broccoli, spinach, rosemary.

Öl
Zucker
Brötchen
Salami
Käse
Joghurt
Eier

In German (found in St. Louis): Oil, sugar, rolls, salami, cheese, yogurt, eggs. You can tell this one is German, because it just looks so darn German!

GATAS
CARNE NORTE
ITLOG
SPAM
TINAPAY
RAMEN
GULAY
ISDA

From the Philippines: This one is fun because Filipino words are fun!

In Polish (found in Chicago): White sausage, unknown, sauerkraut, cake, pound cake.

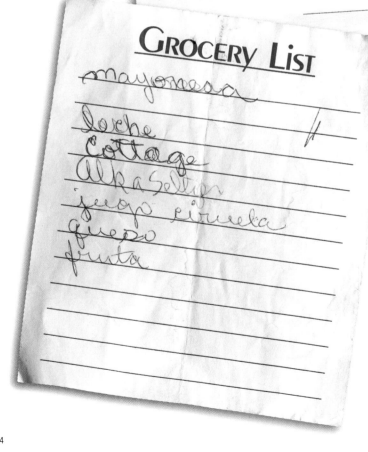

① Biała Kiełbasa
② Ydling
③ Kapusta Kisona
④ Ciasto
⑤ Babka

GROCERY LIST

mayonesa
leche
cottage
Alka Seltzer
jugo ciruela
queso
fruta

In Spanish (found in St. Louis): Mayonnaise, milk, cottage cheese, Alka Seltzer, plum juice, cheese, fruit.

There really was a Hidden Valley Ranch. It was a resort in California, and it was there that ranch dressing was "invented" sometime in the 1950s.

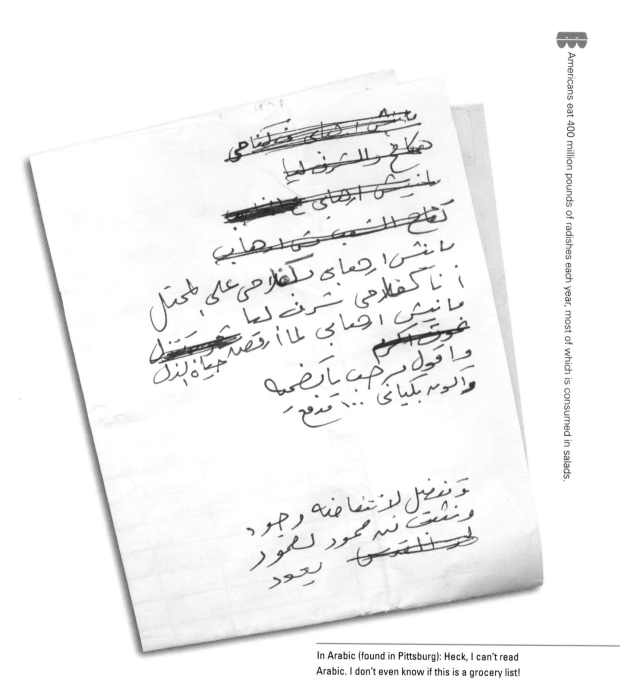

In Arabic (found in Pittsburg): Heck, I can't read
Arabic. I don't even know if this is a grocery list!

The first ready-mix food to be sold commercially was Aunt Jemima pancake flour, introduced in 1889.

Milk
bread.
tins.
cheese.
Bananas
oranges.
turkey
sausages.
carrots
potatoes.
mince
chicken - fillets
biscuits
nappies

From the U.K.: Busted
by "mince and nappies."
Otherwise, a perfectly
basic American list.

Electric refrigerators were first sold to American households in 1916, at a cost of $900.

- yağ.
- çiçek.
- kırmızı şeker.
- cream cheese.
- mayonez.
- vazo.
- koku
- koku kuyacalı.

In Turkish (found in Chicago): Unknown, flower, red sugar, cream cheese, mayonnaise, vase, aroma, unknown aroma.

From parts unknown: Is this an entirely new, as yet unknown, language? Is it code? Or is it just some damn sloppy handwriting?

15.

HEALTHY (AND HYGIENIC) LISTS

or, is that an organic banana in your pocket?

The organic food market is growing rapidly. As we learn more and more about pesticides, preservatives and nutrition, more and more people are choosing to go natural. According to a recent MSNBC report, the organic food industry has seen an annual growth rate of around 17 to 20% over the last several years while the traditional food industry has increased at a rate of just 2 to 3%. But health isn't just about eating the right things. Good hygiene and helpful medicines are important as well. Have a look ...

Oh, you were doing so well! Wheat gluten, wheat germ, lecithin, natural peanut butter and "organic fun stuff." Then we flip over your list and find "lard." Shame on you!

bumble bee bumble bee bumble bee

Whole Foods / ~~Central Market~~

decaf tea
aluminum free baking powder
nat. peanut butter
~~iodized sea salt~~
~~safflower oil~~
~~olive oil~~
~~honey~~
~~brewer's yeast~~ (nutritional yeast)
wheat gluten
wheat germ
lecithin
parmesean cheese
organic fun stuff

The Piggly Wiggly grocery chain started in Memphis, Tennessee in 1916.

"Green stuff"

Fruits that float in Jell-O: fresh fruit such as bananas, citrus sections, sliced peaches, apples and fruit in light syrup.

Turmeric is the root of a tropical plant that has been used in cooking since 600 B.C.

> 4 fat (big) yogurt
> organic broccoli flowerettes
(frozen)

> frozen berries (organic)

I guess frozen organics are better than no organics.

So healthy and chemical free.
This list makes me feel polluted.

fruit/vegii s.

1) 10 apples any kind — organic
2) Brocolli — organic
3) Salad bag — organic.
4) 5 oranges — organic
5) organic grapes.

1) Orange juice, Grape fruit juice
2) ~~fat fee~~ / organic milk fat free
3) Dong's Calorie-free tea
4) organic egg (small ones — 6 eggs inside)
5) In the cafereria area
pick foods you want to eat
for next 2-3 days.

Post Menstrea Douch
medicated Douch
New Downy
3 Panty Hose .

Needed: new pantyhose, laundry detergent and post-menstrual
douche. I get the feeling someone had a very bad day.

In West Virginia, if you hit an animal with your car, you can take it home and cook it for dinner.
A law passed in 1998 lets drivers keep their roadkill, as long as they report it within twelve hours.

Ground beef should be used within two days of purchase. Frozen at 0° F, it will last up to three months.

IS IT ORGANIC?

You don't always have to go to specialty shops or farmer's markets for fresh organic produce. You can tell if the goods have been grown organically by looking at the PLU (Price Look-Up) sticker. Most produce has one of these stickers and if the sticker has a five-digit number that starts with "9," then it's an organic product. If the sticker shows a four-digit number then the produce has been grown using conventional farming methods, which usually include pesticides.

Nobody's getting any sleep in that house.

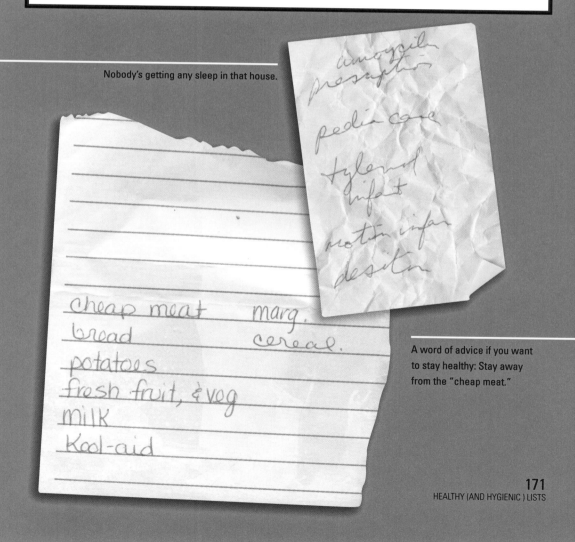

cheap meat   marg.
bread   cereal.
potatoes
fresh fruit, & veg
milk
Kool-aid

A word of advice if you want to stay healthy: Stay away from the "cheap meat."

Quick breads (chemically leavened) were not developed until the end of the 18th century. Up until that time, to make light baked goods, you had to beat air into the dough with eggs or egg whites, or by using yeast (or beer).

WELLNESS FORM
PROTEIN
YOGI TEA
CHAMOMILE
GALA COLON CLEANSE!
SOUP

Gala Colon Cleanser—as if cleaning out your ass was even remotely similar to throwing a giant party.

Herpescin L
Potatoes
Toothpaste
Coffee
Cigarettes French
Creamer French
Vanilla
LYSOL SPRAY
antibactrial

Attacked by viruses AND bacteria. Might as well smoke up.

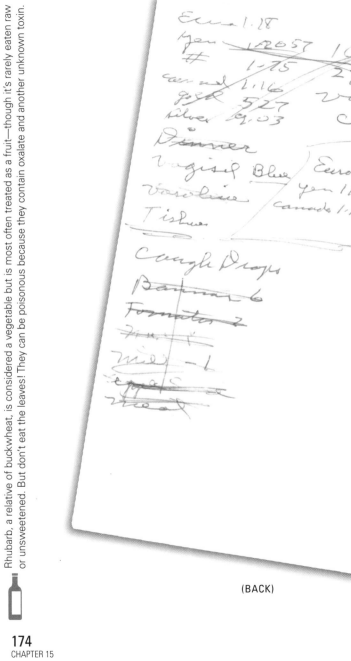

Rhubarb, a relative of buckwheat, is considered a vegetable but is most often treated as a fruit—though it's rarely eaten raw or unsweetened. But don't eat the leaves! They can be poisonous because they contain oxalate and another unknown toxin.

(BACK)

Jicama is the edible starchy, tuberous root of a South American vine of the bean family.

(FRONT)

This is pure speculation, but I imagine it's no
fun to travel the world with an itchy vagina.
Nice vacation photo on the other side, though!

16.

EATING WRONG

nutritional no-nos

Healthy may be good for some, but unhealthy is the choice for most of us. Trans-saturated fats? Yum! Processed foods? More please! Yes, it's no wonder that government studies indicate that approximately 64% of Americans are overweight or obese. That's insane. The Centers for Disease Control reports that the one-two punch of poor nutrition and an inactive lifestyle is quickly catching up with tobacco as a cause of death in the U.S. We eat like crap—and our waistlines, our health and our grocery lists prove it. I'm no exception. I love bad food and I know I should eat better. But at least I don't eat as poorly as these folks. Quick, let's have some chuckles over these unhealthy shopping lists before one of you drops dead.

Buns
Ketchup
Pickles
Cheeze
smokes

You forgot "mustard"
and "coronary."

Canned tuna fish
Paper towels
frozen peas eggs milk
biscuits
Pie crusts
mince for pie
vanilla ice cream
chz in can
crackers soda
meat

No matter what else you have on your
list, the moment you write down "chz
in can" the list becomes unhealthy.

Originally, jerky was wind- and sun-dried strips of llama or buffalo meat. The word comes from the Spanish *charqui* which is from the Quechua Indian word *echarqui*, meaning long thins strips of dried meat.

Hey friend, you're kind of defeating the purpose of shopping at Whole Foods if you're there to buy hot dogs, nuggets, pizzas, fries and fish sticks. Jeez.

whole Foods

- hot dogs
- nuggets
- pizzas
- fries
- spinach
- CA blend
- fish stks
- tuna

- lamb
- steak

- new potatoes
- organic potatoes

Jesse

SHOPPING LIST

- Pop
- Bread
- Cereal
- Juice
- Cookies
- Pizza
- Brownies Mix
- Cheese
- Eggs
- Hotdogs
- Chocolate
- Butter
- Chips

© Martin Designs LTD

Note the conspicuous absence of yucky things like, say, fruits and vegetables.

Liquid diet. Livin' like a rock star.

Busch lite
So Comfort

best served chilled!

Cigs

Nic, gum

dry spagetti

clorox so.wt wend

refills

milk, od, apples,

bananas, lettuce,

tomatos, coke,

tylonol,

soda water

lunch meat, cheese

No, no, no—you have to choose
just one! You can't have cigarettes
AND Nicotine gum!

Bacon is cured and smoked pork. In the U.S. pork bellies are used, Canadian bacon is made from the rib eye of boneless pork loin, and most European countries use the ham (thigh) or shoulder to make bacon.

AGP ®
Ag Processing Inc

Cat treats

TV dinners   GPC cig

scoop away

PO36 9/97

What a sad and lonely life.

Transderm-Nitro® ♥
· nitroglycerin
Winning the hearts of patients *TARGET*
everywhere

SodA
CAwdy
FREbE2E

629-1626-A

Soda and candy. It's a good
thing you already have some
heart medicine lined up.

Meat
cisf
buns
treats

Simple decadence is much more
satisfying than elaborate decadence.

Heart attack. Check.

milk ✓
bread ✓
beer ✓
cigs ✓
hamb ✓
buns ✓
cheese ✓
~~beans~~
mac + cheese ✓

17.

UNSURE OF MYSELF

questions marks and shopping larks

What is the true purpose of the question mark on a grocery list? Does it mean, "Am I sure I want this product?" Or, "Am I sure I need this product?" Or, "Am I sure this product is available at the store?" Or, "Am I sure this product even exists?" Or does it mean, "I sure like the shape of question marks." I don't know. Do you?

Poor Jason, no one remembers when he was born. At least he's going to get some birthday treats.

If you're getting hamburger buns, I'm pretty certain you oughtta get some hamburger too.

B-Day Treat
Josh 25
Jason ?

RAMADA

Yogurt
milk lunch meat
7 up hash browns
hamburger buns   bananas
small garbage bags
Mazola Spray   hamburger
                              ?

spam
Vitamin B & C

Hefty on Zip
soup   Hefty Grip Lock
Pears   Quart

2530 HOLIDAY RD.   CORALVILLE, IA 52241   TEL (319) 354-7770
I-80 EXIT 240   RESV. 1-800-2RAMADA   FAX (319) 337-9002

Nutmeg is unique among spice plants, producing two distinct spices. The seed is dried, shelled and sold either whole or ground as the spice nutmeg. The outer fleshy network is also dried and ground, producing the spice known as mace.

Ice cream
potatoes
glue
flashlets Bulbs   Steel
Bourbon   Pipe

Replace chip

Ten Coffee cups ACB
Sterno + Stove
Ziplocks P+f qts

(BACK)

Kohlrabi is high in fiber, an excellent source of vitamin C and a good source of potassium. It contains about 40 calories per cup.

Yearly losses from stolen, lost and broken shopping carts total $180 million in the U.S.

Ralph thinks to himself, "Hmmmm. Did God tell me to use the knife? Or was it the hatchet?!"

(FRONT)

Heinz sells more than 50% of the ketchup in the U.S. (and 48% of the frozen potatoes).

BE SURE OF YOURSELF:
SOME SMART SHOPPING TIPS

At the risk of having this book actually be useful, here are my top ten tips to help you make the most of going to the grocery store.

1. EAT FIRST: Eat before you go. Hungry shoppers tend to buy things they don't need.

2. PLAN AHEAD: Try planning all your meals out for a week and buy only what you need for those meals. Organize your refrigerator, freezer and cupboards before you go, so when you get home you can quickly put things away. This will also give you the opportunity to do a pre-shopping inventory to make sure you don't buy things you already have.

3. CLIP A LOT: Coupons save money and taking a few minutes each week to clip them can add up to hundreds of dollars per year.

4. TRY GENERIC: Store brand frozen broccoli might cost 40% less than the comparable name brand.

5. BYOB: Bring Your Own Bags. Everyone has stashes of those plastic bags from the grocery store. Sure, they can be used at home or recycled, but it makes environmental sense to get a few large canvas shopping bags and bring them to the store with you each time.

6. STOCKPILE: If a non-perishable item you use frequently is on sale, buy a lot of it.

7. PAY LESS: Watch the weekly circulars. You may find that buying your health and beauty products at a drugstore is cheaper than buying them at the grocery.

8. PAY ATTENTION: Watch the scanner when checking out. Grocery stores only seem to make mistakes that benefit them—meaning when the scanner shows an incorrect price it's almost always an overcharge, not an undercharge. Also, check expiration dates!

Canned food has a shelf life of at least two years from the date of processing.

9. MAKE A LIST: Make a grocery list and stick to it (don't cave in to impulse buys). The time spent making a list will almost certainly be less than the time you might spend going back to the store to pick up something you forgot. Try using the downloadable shopping list I designed as seen in chapter 12.

10. LEAVE BEHIND: Always leave your list in the shopping cart when you're done! Someone might find it and send it to me and I'll have the chance to make fun of you on the Internet and in books. Thank you. Happy shopping!

Coffee
tomato sauce (2)
skim milk
Freezer containers
Yogurt
baking soda/powder?
Granola (AAA)

You really better figure out if it's baking soda or baking powder that you need. The distinction is kind of important.

EXCEL BANK

lunchmt   salad
nuts →swtnd
feta chs
salad drsg.
spinach
cereal
choc milk
cookies?
mt. sub.
insalted nuts

When in doubt, always get the cookies.

SHIEK
SHEIK

Candy
milk
Gold Bond Powder
Hand Soap
Dish Soap
Salmon   3.38
Spam
Pasta Sauce 1.97
Juice?
Toothpaste

Um, how do you spell
sheik? Oh yeah, I need
toothpaste, but I'm not
sure about the juice.

Colby cheese
Dial Gold soap
Miracle Whip
Velveeta
Deodarant
Frozen ?

Frozen fish? Frozen pizzas? Frozen toes? Frozen bank account?

Beer? Yes, get some beer.

MILK
EGGS
EGG BEATERS

GOOD BREAD
KING O'HILL
Chicky tenders

GR BEEF

BACON BITS

Shay cream

RAGU

WINE
Beer?

CANNED DOG FOOD

I SAID GET SOME BEER.
WHAT'S THE PROBLEM?

Potatoe Chips
~~Rainbow Sherbet~~
Rainbow Sherbet
Anything more
2 Kraft Dressings
= Salad
Lemons
Lunch meat

Beer?

LIQUOR

~~BANANAS~~

H2O Melon
New Potatoes
Strawberry Ice Cream
or Sherbet?

K-Mart - Shoes 6W (KI)?
√ for markdowns?

Paint? NO√   √ Hobby Lobby?

If nearly everything on your list has
a question mark after it, what the hell
are you trying to get done?

18.

OTHER LISTS
to-do lists, et cetera

As I mentioned in the introduction, lists are a big part of our culture. Grocery lists are just a small subset of the plentiful bizarre and useful lists we make. To-do lists probably rule our lives, even more than grocery lists. Everyone has things to do and most of us get a feeling of accomplishment by writing those things down and crossing them off. But some of us just accomplish making strange lists.

Artichokes actually are a large, unopened flower bud.

INGUINAL REGION
- INGUINAL CANAL — INDIRECT INGUINAL HERNIA
- ANTERIOR SUPERIOR ILIAC SPINE
- PELVIC GIRDLE
- PELVIC INLET

10/01/04

- SWISS MISS W/ MARSH
- COFFEEMATE X
- DETERGEN X
- BLEACH X
- INSTANT COFFEE X
- CONDOMS X
- TOOTHBRUSH X
- CHIPS X
- CORN OIL X
- CUP NOODLES X
- CAMPBELLS
- SHAMPOO X
- BEER X
- BREAD X

FUCK

Grocery/etc. list: A bit of grocery shopping, a bit of groin-oriented medical terminology, and just a tiny bit of the F-word.

Lipton's dry Onion Soup Mix was introduced in 1952, and soon became a common ingredient in hundreds of recipes.

Shopping list: Oh my. I want to work where she works!

Wal-Mart:

Stockings

undergarments
(for work-possibly
w/ red stripper shoes)

Make up Guest Bedroom
Scan Comp for Virus
Scan Disc - Fix Errors
Defrag
Luncheon
Eye Doc Appt
Fix dinner < Meat Loaf?
              Chicken Thing?

To-do list: The price you pay for using a PC. And having friends. And needing to eat.

Larson
PRINTING CO.

714 S Delaware Ave
P.O. Box 380
Mason City IA 50401
Ph 641-424-2623
Fx 641-424-8465
larsonpr@netconix.net
www.larsonprinting.net

Electronic Film Output
Typeset & Layout
Full Color Printing
Quick Printing
Color Copies
High Speed Copying
Bindery & Finishing
Large Laminating
USPS Certified Mailer

Full Service Printing . . . Our Only Business

Walmart
dog
money order

DVD Kmart
Par Entertainm min VCR Tapes
Mall coffee

Shopko
VCR tape ← Comforter
Calendar
Hu - Drugtown

Shopping list: "I'm going to Wal-Mart to get a money order. And a dog."

GAS

Reminder list: I guess this one's pretty self-explanatory.

SCOOP

(BACK)

CIG
SAT – 6
SON – 5
M – 5
M – 4
T – 4
W – 4
T – 2   1 – 1130 – A – 2 ND 7½
                              LATER
          21 @ – 2H @5
F – ½ 2
S – 1
S – 1
M – 1
T – – 1
W – 1
T – 2

(FRONT)

Tomato catsup has a high acid content (due to both the tomatoes and vinegar in it) so it does not have to be refrigerated. It is safe to store it at room temperature, but it will taste better if kept refrigerated.

Daily cigarette list: "Ever since I've been trying to quit smoking I've been craving GIANT SCOOPS OF ICE CREAM. I wonder if they make Nicotine flavored?"

Eggplants are native to India. The name refers to an earlier white-skinned variety.

CHANCING UPON CHEVY

Here's a letter and list (see next page) I received from a grocerylists.org reader from New York. She had a great story, so I figured I'd let her tell it in her own words.

Dear Bill,

Written on the back of this expense list for taking care of a quadriplegic bound in a wheelchair is Chevy Chase's autograph. At the time it was signed, a friend of mine was caretaker for the quadriplegic and brought him to a Yankee game. He used this piece of cardboard to keep track of what he spent that day so he could be reimbursed. Well, in the restroom at Yankee Stadium, Kyle was peeing and heard the crowd begin yelling. He looked around for a TV thinking a good play had just happened when he saw a tall guy with sunglasses on, wearing a baseball cap. Not a Yankees cap, more Field & Stream. It was Chevy Chase, relieving himself beside Kyle!

　　Kyle then said, "Shit, no home run!," Followed quickly by "I loved you in the *Vacation* movies." Chevy quickly signed the only item Kyle had in his pocket—the list of expenses—smirked, and left the bathroom.

　　Just think—Chevy didn't even wash his hands before signing this! How cool yet gross! I picked this out of Kyle's garbage (also gross?) because he was going to throw it away!

Best regards,

Kristine Rakowsky
New York, New York

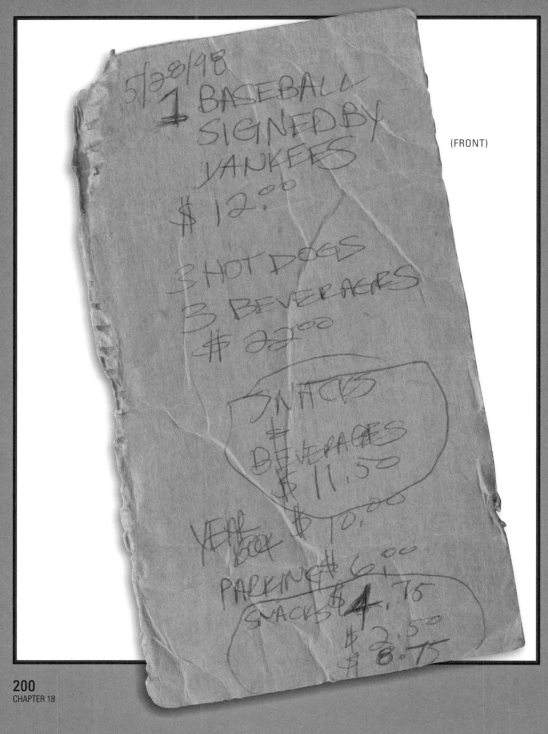

(FRONT)

A refrigerator temperature of 40° F or less slows the growth of most bacteria. The temperature won't kill the bacteria, but it will keep them from multiplying, and the fewer there are, the less likely you are to get sick.

(BACK)

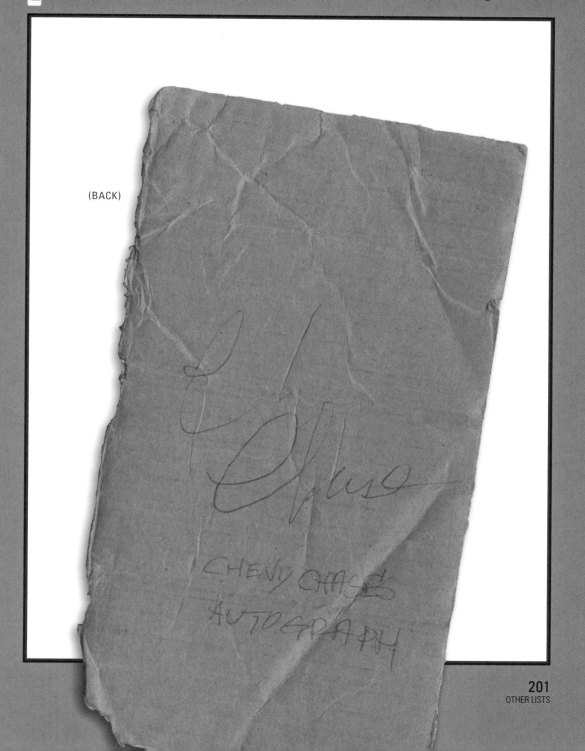

CHEVY CHASES
AUTOGRAPH

ED

Shop N Save
WAll Stay the Same
Lay's
POD Display
MON Super Size
Ruffles/Tostitos

END CAP
Doritos
Tostito
Melt
Eay

Schnucks (Q)   South City
4 ft
Sun
Day   Lobby → Lay's   END CAP Tostitos
Tostitos   BND Grill   Tost Imp   Doritos
✓ ?

ASK DAN   Schnucks A
Lobby Lays   END CAP Tostitos
Sunday   ?itos
or Doritos → ✓
Lays   Tost itos   ✓ ?

Planning list: This seems to be a list and diagram for setting up the endcap displays in a
supermarket. I know you're thinking, "Who gives a crap." But this is one of the ways they get
you to make impulse buys. This sketch is probably, like, a classified grocery store document.

Gift list: Jeez, organize some sort of
holiday gift swap. It sucks buying
something for everyone you work with.

BRILLIANCE

Buy Xmas gift for office

(10)

Lynne   Mary Jane
Brenda   John
Abby   Vanessa
               Brenda
               Sue
               Julie
               Joanna

When a collection of brilliant minds, hearts,
and talents come together...
a masterpiece.

Kylee ~~~~~~~
Sub Folder
Kitten Faces
Wands
MEE

Shopping list: Kitten faces! No!!!!! (I'm told this is probably a
supply list for an early childhood special education teacher.)

RECEPTIONIST - GRAPHICS WORLD
FAX RES TO 314-567-7178

CLERK - UPSCALE ADULT RETAIL
314-588-7873 - CALL

(✓) ADMIN ASST.
THE ARTHUR WELLS GROUP
(SENT) ATTN: NLI - A/A
FAX 314-264-5714
HRDEPT@ THE AWGROUP.com

(SENT) ACCT COORDINATOR
INQ@ COMMERCIAL - LETTER.com

ADMIN ASST
FLEISHMANN'S YEAST
SAL REQ - EMPLOYMENT@ BANA.com

Job-hunt list: Sending out resumes and looking through the classifieds and job posting sites = No Fun.

Reminder list: For a day out on the lake—what else could a guy need (besides maybe pants)?

City of Cleveland

Department of Port Control
Cleveland Hopkins International Airport
5300 Riverside Drive
Cleveland, Ohio 44135-3193
216/265-6000 • FAX 216/265-6096

Sunglasses

Shoes

Beer

$

Food

Some call edamame (immature green soybeans) a super-vegetable because it's the only veggie that contains all nine essential amino acids. This makes edamame a complete protein source, similar to meat or eggs.

Snapple Iced Tea was introduced in 1987 and the ready-to-drink iced tea category exploded.

Thanksgiving responsibility list: The grandma always gets stuck making the banana cake. Because who else would know how to make a banana cake?

3 California
3 Spicy Tuna
1 Oi Shinko
1 Takkamaki
2 Ebi
2 Sake
2 Hamachi
2 Maguro
1 Spicy Roll
1 Tempura Roll
1 Rainbow

Sushi order list: Mmmmmmm. I could
go for some sushi right now too.

Christmas or birthday wish list: So what do you think he got? Probably the books. I mean, he did ask for books.

MY List

1. ~~Mote the~~
1. Model train set
2. model boats
3. remote control model airplane
4. Lego set
5. books
6. Mini ipod silver

Most fruit juices begin to taste a little stale after a few days. Aerate to revive the taste by pouring it back and forth a few times, or fill a blender and turn it on for a few seconds.

To-do list: This just makes me laugh. Haw-haw-haw!

19.

ALL-AMERICAN LISTS
the lost grocery lists of America

When I started working on this book, I thought it would be interesting to include a list from every U.S. state. Although I only had about half of what I needed, I put out requests and grocerylists.org readers came through. (Yay!) So here I present to you, in all their flag-waving, bread-buying glory, fifty lists from fifty states (plus Washington D.C.).

Eggplants are actually fruits, and are classified botanically as berries.

Alabama
```
0,CD
CWA
CN
Bread (sandwich)
- Printer
- Frigidaire
```

Arizona
```
Bananas, ber
Carrots, Ce
chicken broth
raisin bran
total? Wh
```

Alaska
```
Romaine lettuce
Broccoli
Sugar snap peas
Edamame
Garlic
Parmesean Cheese (not in a bottle)
Pine nuts
Almonds
Tofu
Rice noodles
Balsamic vinegar
Mayonnaise
Fresh shrimp
French Silk ice cream
Soy milk
Chocolate
Diet Coke
12-grain bread
Kashi cereal
```

Arkansas
```
2 ·block bags
dinner stuff
shredded cheese
chili
Sour cream
milk
```

California
```
flour
celery
andouille
Chicken
```

Colorado
```
Pan cake M
Dish Soap
tolit Papper
coffee
```

Connecticut
```
Salt
Hot Cocoa
Meat
apples
```

Delaware
```
Bananas
Apples
Oranges
2%, 1/2 gal
Entenmanns
```

Florida
```
Laundry Det.
Clorex wipes
hair spray
Sugar
```

Georgia
```
5) Eggplant (if in good co
6) Carrots (2lb)
7) Scallions
8) Olive oil
9) Fresh spinach (Columbu
10) Water chestnuts (2 ca
11) Baby corn (1 can)
12) red radish or daikon
13) hubbard or kobacha sq
14) cat litter
15) light bulbs (40 watt)
16) Really good bleu chees
17) Roast sunflower seeds
only)
18) Bad karma pickles (Co
```

Hawaii
```
AA batteries
pork tenderloin
bread crumbs
butter (unsal-
cornmeal
```

Idaho

Produce:		Dry/Pasta
bag salad		rice
carrots		mac & ch
celery		lasagna
bananas		spaghett
tomatoes		
apples		taco she
onions		taco sea
potatoes		Other:
		box juice
Soups:		V-8 juice
cheese		soda
bean w/bacon		
crm. Mushroom		Dairy:

Illinois
```
• O.J.
• fruit
• crackers
• romaine lettuce
```

Indiana
```
Pop Tarts    hot do
             salsa
Oatmeal      Chips
Sugar        Instant
Bologna      Mashed pot.
Donuts       pizza
Ham burger
```

Iowa
```
48
12   36
     54
full flavor
Ice cream
chicken soup
```

Brown gargle: Cowboy slang for coffee.

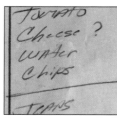

Kansas

Tomato
Cheese ?
water
Chips

TEAS

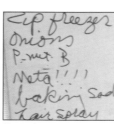

Kentucky

zip freezer
onions
P-nut B
Meat !!!!
baking soda
hair spray

Louisiana

onions
gr. onions
bell pepper

maple syrup
Dijon mustard
yellow must

Maine

MILK
LUBE

Nevada

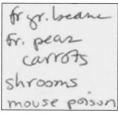

Maryland

fr gr. beans
fr. peas
carrots
shrooms
mouse poison

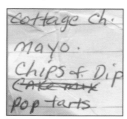

Massachusetts

cottage ch.
mayo.
Chips & Dip
CAKE MIX
pop tarts

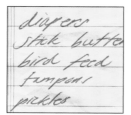

Michigan

diapers
stick butter
bird feed
tampons
pickles

Minnesota

DUCT TAPE
LINUS HAIR
COLLEGE
WRESTLING SCHOOL

Mississippi

popcorn
alfalfa tablets
Fig Bars and alike
Salsa
Almond butter
Apple juice
Tempeh
Whole wheat spaget
(Organic pasta)
Sandwich meats

Missouri

! list !
x orang
x red pepp
x 2 portabe
mushroo
x basi

Montana

vinegar
bacon
pudding
butter

Nebraska

lipstick-free
makeup?
hanes classic-
me PJs
Julia books
Easter placemats

eat treats
Dog treats NO
BAD DOG!
eggs
soymilk ✓B.D.
salad stuff
feta
Choco. raisins ☐
almonds
lemons x 2
cott. ch.
spinach
lemon
baby eggplants (recipe pg 84)

☐ a life - check
aisle 14
keep looking.

Americans eat 18.3 pounds of onions every year, per capita.

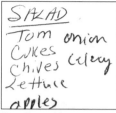

SALAD
Tom onion
Cukes celery
chives celery
Lettuce
apples

New Hampshire

DRINKS
☐ milk
☐ cereal (raisin brand,
☐ cokes (diet coke, die
☐ crystal light
☐ juice (orange, lime)

New Mexico

sugar cookie log
spinach
ricotta
lasagna pasta strips
salad stuff
phish phood
strawberries
peaches
FP [Sale]
soda
coffee
dog food*
milk

bread mstre.
turkey
swiss
hard roll

YELLOW.

New Jersey

Chicken Thigh
Liverwurst.

New York

Absolut vodka
2 bot. cab. sa
KJ chardona
tomatoes

North Carolina

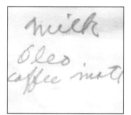

milk
Oleo
coffee mat

North Dakota

[PIG]
1) BLUE BONNET
2) MILK
3) HEINZ KETCHUP
4) G.E. APPLESAUC

Ohio

garlic powder
tips coffee
koho sat
WINDEX
Bread
MILK
BOLOGNA

Oklahoma

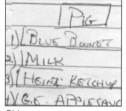

milk
Salsa
Cereal
H. Food

Oregon

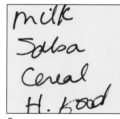

TUNA
Gr meat
chicken Brea
Roast
cheese - G
Lunch mea

Pennsylvania

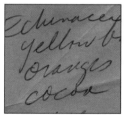

Echinacey
yellow b
oranges
cocoa

Rhode Island

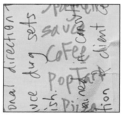

oral direction
savor
ce drug sets
Cofee
client
PopTart
sh.
Pizza

South Carolina

Meds 4 me & C
Pick up my Gla
Gas
WINE
0.28

South Dakota

Milk
Popcorn   Chicken
Bread   Pepper (+
Peanut butter   salt
Yogurt   Fruit
Pudding
Turkey

Tennessee

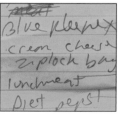

Blue kleenex
cream cheese
ziplock bag
lunchmeat
Diet pepsi

Texas

213

🍾 Unopened beer has a shelf live of about four months.

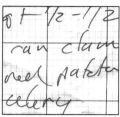

Utah

Grapefruit Juice
& herb
Stuffing

Vermont

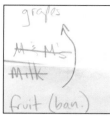

grapes
M&M's
Milk
fruit (ban.)

Virginia

Washington

mustard   milk   2 hoa
mayosie cereal   18 ut
Ketups 2cheeg   4 b r
Cabich 6 hotdogs   2 lb S
Beans
Potatoes 3 sausge   1 Stak
use noddle note 2 Soup   1 old
6 Spam   1 crackers   Sor
2 mix veg dble btunar   1 ro
3 dozen eggs pickles   1 ro

West Virginia

[ ] Jell-O
[ ] Meat T H B P O
[ ] Pita Bread
[ ] Salads_____

BAKERY
[ ] Bread
[ ] Buns Ham Hot
[ ] Rolls H O
[ ] Misc.

Wisconsin

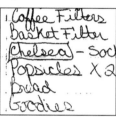

Coffee Filters
Basket Filter
Chelsea - Soc
Popsicles X 2
Bread
Goodies

Wyoming

_____

Washington, D.C.

A FEW FACTS ABOUT THESE ALL-AMERICAN LISTS

Although I've cropped these lists due to space considerations, I studied and parsed them beforehand. Here are the stats:

- 41% list a bread product
- 37% list milk
- About ⅓ list some sort of cleaning or personal care product
- Almost ¼ of them include a misspelling
- 12% list bananas
- Just 6% list some type of alcohol (yeah, right)
- Only one person was shopping for ginger ale
- Just one person needed "milk and lube"

milk
sugar
Bread
coffee + creamer
spaghetti + sauce
Broccoli
squash potatoes
ground beef
Fish sticks
Hot Dogs
Chicken
French Fries
Frz vegs
Cn milk
Pork + beans
Kidney Beans

20.

WHAT'S COOKIN'?

recipes made using

other people's grocery lists

Normally, I don't eat things I find on the ground, but occasionally I make exceptions. Especially when I find a list on the ground—and it features a selection of delicious items that can be made into a meal. (Note: Don't eat the list itself—just use it for shopping!) For this project, I challenged my wife to create a meal from things other people wrote on their grocery lists. She wanted to use the list that read, "Spaghetti, spaghetti sauce, garlic bread" but I said no. So she came up with broiled salmon served over a bed of sautéed leeks in a kicky jalapeno cream sauce. Huzzah! Here is a day's worth of yummy meals concocted from five discarded grocery lists. For the most part, these meals use items found on a particular list but a little shopping and/or cupboard rummaging might be required to make sure the meal doesn't suck. Enjoy!

Cucumbers are about 95% water, and have very little nutritional value.

Start your day right: french toast with brown sugar peaches and yogurt cheese.

BREAKFAST: FRENCH TOAST WITH BROWN SUGAR PEACHES AND YOGURT CHEESE

1 cup vanilla yogurt

4 large eggs slightly beaten

1 cup milk

8 slices thick bread

4 medium peaches, pitted and sliced

1/3 cup packed brown sugar

butter

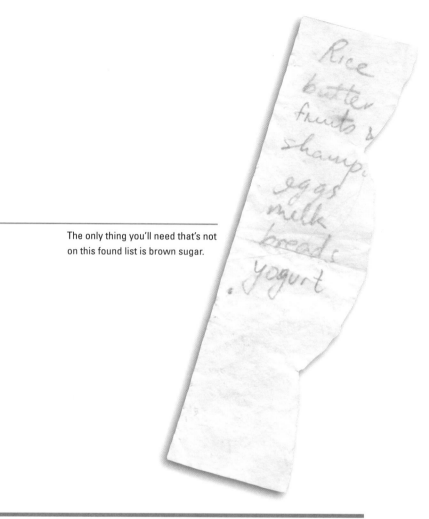

The only thing you'll need that's not on this found list is brown sugar.

According to U.S. Food & Drug Administration regulations, ground paprika is allowed up to 20% mold, 75 insect fragments and 11 rodent hairs per 25 grams, and tomato puree may contain 9 fly eggs and 1 maggot per 100 grams.

The night before, strain yogurt through two paper coffee filters placed in a strainer. The next day, whisk the eggs and milk in a shallow dish. Dip both sides of the bread into the egg mixture and cook on a large buttered skillet. Cook through, until brown on each side. Meanwhile place the sliced peaches and brown sugar in a heavy, two-quart saucepan. Cook until the sugar melts and the peaches are warm. Spoon peach mixture on top of the French toast. Add a large dollop of yogurt cheese. Serves four.

Iceberg lettuce got its name from the fact that California growers started shipping it covered with heaps of crushed ice in the 1920s. It had previously been called crisphead lettuce.

LUNCH: MEDITERRANEAN TUNA SANDWICH

1 round loaf of crusty bread

1/4 cup extra virgin olive oil

2 teaspoons lemon juice or red wine vinegar

1 tomato, sliced

1 6-once can tuna in oil, drained

1/2 cup sliced black olives

1/4 cup chopped onions

1/2 cucumber (diced, seeds removed)

1 hard-boiled egg, sliced

Salt and pepper to taste

A classic with a twist:
Mediterranean tuna sandwich.

Cut bread crosswise. Pull out much of the soft interior, leaving a bread shell. In a small bowl, mix the oil, lemon juice, salt and pepper. Brush cut sides of bread with the oil mixture. Add a layer of tomatoes. In a bowl, mix tuna, cucumber, onions and olives. Scoop over the tomatoes. Add a layer of egg then the remaining tomatoes. Pour the remainder of the dressing on top. Cover with the lid of the bread. Wrap in aluminum foil and refrigerate for a couple of hours to combine the flavors. Cut into wedges. Serves four.

These items are not on this person's list, but you probably have them on hand: Olive oil, lemon juice, salt and pepper.

Eggs x 2
milk (vit d : 2%)
grapes
bread
cereal
tuna fish
cookies
OJ
Rigatoni
Spag. sause
tomato puree
greens
meatballs
cucumbers
salad mix
garlic bread
flour
7-up
Sausage links
onions
garbage bags

Taco's

lettuce
tomatoes
cheese (shredded)
tortilla chips
taco shells
taco seasoning
taco sause
sour cream
ground meat
black olives

Fish with a kick: broiled salmon on a bed of jalapeno leek cream.

DINNER: BROILED SALMON WITH JALAPENO LEEK CREAM

2 tablespoons olive oil plus additional oil to brush on salmon

3 small leeks (halved, washed and sliced—just the white
   and light green sections)

1 jalapeno pepper, finely chopped

1 cup heavy cream

4 salmon fillets

Kosher salt and pepper to taste

Preheat broiler. Heat oil over medium heat in a 12-inch skillet. Add leeks and the jalapeno and cook 15 minutes until soft, stirring occasionally. Stir in heavy cream and cook until slightly reduced. Add salt and pepper to taste. Meanwhile brush each salmon filet with oil and sprinkle with salt. Broil until cooked through, about 8 to 10 minutes. Place salmon on a bed of leeks. Serves four.

Again, you'll just have to get some olive oil, salt and pepper from your cupboard because those basics aren't on this list.

Apple sauce.
Paper napkins.
Tropicana (3) flavers.
coffe ice cream.
chicken cutlets.
American cheese
Tomato sauce.
Diet Pepsi
Nude side water
9 volt bateries
garlic Bread.
block cheese.
Grapes
~~~~~~~~~
Red Potato
leeks.
Donuts.
Metal Pans.
Hunelon.

Pigs in Blanket
Cumin.
garlic.
2# Beef tend
butter milk.
andray fillets.
Jalepno.
Cheddar.
Tomatoes.
Sprouts.
Shallots.
3# Salmon fillet.
Strawberries.
grana cracker crust
2quart Strawberries.
6 pint heavy cream.
Strawberry seedless.
No

DESSERT: CHEESECAKE WITH PORT-SOAKED CRANBERRIES

For cake:

1 pound cream cheese, softened

1 cup sugar

1 teaspoon vanilla

3 large eggs

1 premade graham cracker pie shell

For topping:

1 cup sour cream

1/4 cup sugar

1 teaspoon vanilla

For sauce:

1/2 cup port

1 teaspoon sugar

1 cup cranberries

Decadent and delicious: cheesecake with port-soaked cranberries.

Preheat oven to 350° F. Beat cream cheese on medium speed until smooth. Add sugar, vanilla and eggs. Beat five minutes. Pour cream cheese mixture into shell and place in oven. Cook 45 minutes or until center is almost set. Cool on a wire rack. Meanwhile combine sour cream, vanilla and sugar. Spread sour cream mixture on top of cheesecake. Cool cheesecake completely. In a one-quart saucepan, cook port and sugar over a medium-low heat for about 15 minutes or until reduced in half. Remove from heat. Add cranberries and let stand. Refrigerate for three hours while port mixture cools. Serve cheesecake with a spoonful of cranberry mixture. Serves six.

There are a few important items not on the discarded list (sugar, vanilla, port) but this cheesecake is so delicious I'm sure you'll forgive me.

A delicious fall beverage: the pumpkin milkshake.

The inside of a cucumber can actually be up to 20° F cooler than the outside temperature.

DRINK: PUMPKIN MILKSHAKE

1/2 cup evaporated milk

2 scoops vanilla ice cream

1/2 teaspoon pumpkin pie spice

1/4 cup pureed pumpkin

Blend ingredients in blender until smooth. Serves one.

PAPER TOWELS
ICE CREAM / CONES
DR. PEPPER
PUMPKIN — 1 CAN
EVAP MILK
PUMPKIN SPICE

You'll find everything you need on this list.

EPILOGUE

Whew. Now we're done. No wait, there's more: I run a web site at www.grocerylists.org which is, of course, the world's largest online collection of found grocery lists. This book features about 200 of the best, but you can see a couple thousand more on the site. If you want to be part of this project you can contribute yours or any lists you find at the store by e-mailing scans to bill@grocerylists.org. Who knows, I may do another book someday—so if you want your contribution considered for publication please send the actual lists to:

Grocerylists.org
P.O. Box 752
St. Louis, MO 63188

And remember, if you eat baby meat that means you are a cannibal. So don't eat baby meat. The end.

227

INDEX

228

229

231